A

THE WILD FLOWERS OF
DUNSTANBURGH

By Don Banbury

First published in Great Britain as a softback original in
2013

Copyright © Don Banbury 2013

The moral right of this author has been asserted.

Typeset in Gentium Book Basic and Alice

Design and publishing by Consilience Media

www.consil.co.uk
ISBN: 978-0-9926433-0-0

Foreword from the National Trust

Like many a child growing up in Newcastle in the 1950's I holidayed locally. With no car in the family Mam, Dad, sister and I went where the bus would take us, so Craster and Seahouses were summer destinations. I well remember playing in the dunes or on the beach and being dragged, not always willingly, along to Dunstanburgh Castle and beyond. My Dad, a physics teacher by trade and a naturalist at heart, would always point out the wild flowers on our walks. Looking back, some of his identification may have been a bit dodgy but, to be fair, guide books were few and far between - and the illustrations were in black and white!

Those early excursions obviously had an effect on me as, for the past thirty years or so, this has been my professional 'patch'. Working for the National Trust, both on the Farne Islands and on the Coast have come to know this area intimately - and what a great place it is. Part of the attraction is the variety of the wild flowers to be seen, and this guide is a brilliant introduction. The variety is down to the underlying rock type, the soils, proximity to the coast, the weather, and some careful management. As Don writes in his introduction, Dunstanburgh Golf Course is 'situated on National Trust terrain'. All the land is subject to a management plan which is reviewed annually. It is a tribute to the management and staff of the Club, and the National Trust rangers, that his superb links course can also be a haven for a variety of wildlife and wild flowers. If you are reading this as a golfer try not to curse when you hit into the rough - it's there for a purpose!

Whilst my work requires me to identify wild flowers, I have always been as interested, if not more so, in the folklore and the uses of plants. I thought I was well read on the subject but Don has come up with some fascinating snippets that had eluded me. Do not just use this as an identification guide – it is so much more. There is a 'disclaimer' at the end of the introduction, but I think one safe bet is that dock leaves do ease the pain of stinging nettles – it worked for me fifty odd years ago and still works today.

Read this guide, walk the coast (much of it in the care of the National Trust), play golf, admire the scenery, enjoy the wild flowers – and cherish the fact that you're in such a fabulous part of the world.

John Walton

National Trust

Coastal and Marine Officer

May 2013

Foreword from the Dunstanburgh Castle Golf Course

The flowers of Dunstanburgh are a magnificent and unforgettable spectacle! Sixty years on I still remember my delight at seeing the Cowslips, Orchids and Bloody Cranesbill covering the banks next to the golf course when I visited Embleton as a schoolboy from Newcastle. In the succeeding years I have observed and admired the numerous different species of flower but never learned the names of more than a tiny fraction. Now at last I can find them in this splendid book!

Since those early days I have come to have a greater involvement with the flora at Dunstanburgh. In 1987 I took over as proprietor of Dunstanburgh Castle Golf Course under a lease from the National Trust. The lease boundary enclosed not only the fairways but also areas of golf course rough on which grew many wild flowers. The National Trust was concerned that under the terms of the lease that there were not sufficient provisions to protect the flowers on the terrain. Accordingly, I indicated that I was interested in negotiating a new lease with provisions to protect and enhance these flowers and other features of the Dunstanburgh links. Several years of discussions ensued between me and the National Trust staff before a new lease was signed. These discussions about a new lease were quite detailed and lengthy. On the one hand I had to ensure that nothing interfered with the playing of golf on the historic Dunstanburgh Castle Golf Course – designed by the famous golf course architect, James Braid. On the other hand the National Trust had to ensure the optimum environment was maintained for the wild flowers within the lease boundary. In the end we found that there was little or no conflict between our respective objectives. Whilst there is occasional grumbling by some golfers about the state of the rough, in general the delightful wild flowers are enjoyed by golfers as much as by the others who come to see them. On the part of the National Trust it recognises that many of the wild flowers would not thrive without a golf course being there: the cutting of grass to different lengths on the fairways, semi-rough and rough assists the growth of a wide variety of these flowers! Other provisions in the lease on spraying chemicals etc also ensure maximum protection for the flowers.

My congratulations to Don Banbury on producing this excellent guide! This book will be a delight for all those who – like me – have admired the beautiful wild flowers of Dunstanburgh without knowing their names or the wealth of other information he provides.

Peter Gilbert

Proprietor

Dunstanburgh Castle Golf Course

Acknowledgments

In no particular order I wish to thank Professor Colin Biott, for his valuable guidance; Gustav Macleod MBE for his reading through and correcting my grammar, Robbie Jamieson, Alan Hale (Spike), Peter Lewis and son Nick. Nick for the introduction to John Walton from the National Trust who has written a foreword in this book. Robbie is the head gardener at Howick Gardens, just five minutes' drive from Dunstanburgh. The gardens are well worth a visit to see a wide selection of plants from all corners of the globe. To Dr. Peter Gilbert, the proprietor of Dunstanburgh Castle Golf Course for his insight into the discussions that were held with the National Trust to ensure the protection of the wild flora to ensure a lease for the Golf Club. To my fellow golfers I also wish to thank for having to put up with nature study lessons during their rounds of golf. Sorry I bored you. Also to all those who have helped me with the wizardry of computers. You know who you are. Finally, my wife Vicki for reading through and her constructive ideas.

Introduction

Being a member of Dunstanburgh Golf Club for many years I have often bored my companions by pointing out one or two wild flowers, many of which are illustrated in this book. The sole purpose of this small volume is to kindle an interest in our wild flora, and if this achieved then the job is done. There are many well written books about the Wild Flowers of Britain and Europe, with far more flowers than I have ever seen, so if that interest in the identification has been kindled these are the books for you.

The Golf course is situated on National Trust terrain and the abundance and variety of wild flowers in this relatively small area is quite remarkable. It is a links course so there is the shore line which has its own species of plants, but the area also includes salt marshes, fresh water ponds and streams, rocks and pools, stable sand dunes and even a small area of woodland. All this backs on to agricultural farmland. It is probably not unique for a Golf Course to have such a diversity of habitats where a variety of flora can thrive but there are unlikely to be many. It is not a technical book, but the interest lies in why such a flower is so called and what uses it had in bygone days. Many plants are still used in the kitchen and medicinally today. The Foxglove for example. The drug digitalis is extracted for heart ailments. A basic knowledge of plants is useful. Petals, Sepals, Stamens, Stigma, Ovary and Anthers are as good a start to the botanical parts of plants as any. Most technical books describing flowers will have a glossary of botanical terms.

Although the book is entitled Flowers of Dunstanburgh, it was the intention to illustrate only the flowers growing within the defined boundaries of the Golf Course, but the North East Coast, especially from Warkworth to Holy Island, attracts thousands of visitors each year so it would have been a miss not to include many others that are found in this coastal stretch. However, most of the photographs have been taken within a five mile radius or so of the Dunstanburgh Castle Golf Club House. The exception is the worthwhile visit to Holy Island. Among others we have the Sea Aster, the Marsh Helleborine, the Vipers Bugloss, and the Grass of Parnassus. The selection of flowers is selective and includes the most common flowers many of which will be found in most of Britain. It is not intended to be a technical guide for the identification of flowers, but for all you walkers, ramblers and golfers perhaps at some time you have looked back and just wondered for a moment what and maybe why that flower was so called. If that is so this book might just help. To help an initial identification the plants have been put in an order of their colour.

There are many flowers which are similar in appearance. The Forget-me-Not family and the Parsleys for example, have many similar variances so for simplicity have only included the most common. The Orchid family is numerous. Included here are a few of the most common, seen in this area, but throughout the country where the habitat suits there are dozens of specimens that are well worth 'seeking out'. The Butterfly Orchid, the Bee, the Man, the Monkey, and the Fly Orchid are but just some. There are many more. The Lady's Slipper Orchid was recently discovered in the Yorkshire Dales, a very rare find indeed. There are many grasses which have not been included, but common around the coastline of Britain is the Marram Grass, much responsible for stabilising the dunes from erosion.

Finally, please be aware that the writings in this book are for information only and are no way a guide or prescription for use. Please seek expert advice from qualified personnel before any use whatsoever. The author is not qualified to recommend the use of any of these plants either for food or for the treatment of any medical disorder.

For those interested, all photographs were taken using a Nikon Coolpix 16 Megapixel camera.

Don Banbury

Bindweed

Also known by the descriptive name of Devil's Guts, its
quick growing stems can wrap around any plant that
it comes into contact with and just about strangles
that plant to death. It has far reaching and quick
growing stems well exceeding 200cm that scramble
and attach themselves to any convenient support; the
stems entwining anti-clockwise completing a complete
revolution in less than two hours. Its botanical name is
Convolvulus arvensis, both Latin words. The former word
meaning to twine and the latter relating to cultivated
ground. As might be expected it is an intrusive plant,
and to eradicate it has proved to be difficult. It has an
extensive horizontal root system and as similar with
many of the Thistles, any root left in the soil after

... Bindweed

attempts to dig it up will regenerate. The roots can persist many years in poor soils, but does not like wet or waterlogged areas. Reproduction is by these creeping roots and seed dispersal. However, it is an attractive colourful plant growing on farmland and waste sites. It is a delicate shade of lilac with broad white stripes on the funnel shaped petals and arrow like leaves. Sea Bindweed can be found in gassy areas by the sea. This variety does not climb but has sprawling stems and has kidney shaped leaves. Both these flowers can be seen from June onwards.

Blackberry

Botanically it is not a berry but known as an aggregate fruit of numerous drupelets, meaning that the Blackberry is made up tiny round berries each containing its own seed. Birds and animals feeding off this plant give it a certain guarantee to prolificate. It is one of the 'free foods' we know so well of the countryside

which we all recognise with its arched prickly stems which grow in excess of 5 metres, There are many varieties or micro species, 2000 or more, and it will take an expert in this sphere to differentiate. It survives in many habitats, common in hedgerows woods and scrub. Folklore claims that Blackberries should not be picked after Old Michaelmas Day, the 11th October, because by then the devil has claimed the plant by leaving marks on the leaves by urinating or spitting. It is argued that this could be something to do with the weather. The Blackberry is host to the Shield Bug which, as the name suggests, this bug shields its young from predators by herding them to the underside of the leaf while she gallantly stands guard above. Rubus fruiticosus is its wonderful sounding botanical name, Rubus being its Latin plant name and fruiticosus meaning shrubby.

Bladder Campion

This plant can be seen all around the coast and as the photograph shows it is easily identified by its five deeply notched petals and an exagerated inflated (bladdery) calyx, likenened to an angler's float. It has a waxy greyish green look to its foliage, the leaves being opposite and pointed. Its botanical name is Siline vulgaris, both Latin names, the first being the plants name and the species name meaning common. As late as the 19th century the leaves have been eaten as a vegetable supposedly tasting and smelling of fresh peas. The Bladder Campion, which is a member of the Pink family, likes drier ground, and does not like competition from taller plants. It has a clove like scent which attracts night flying moths and indeed the plant is pollinated by long tongued bees and moths, but curiously the Bumble Bee will settle on the petals and bite through the base of the flower to extract the nectar. This does not help pollination at all. You can see the plant from May onwards.

Branched Bur Reed

They are also known as Puddle plants. The green keepers of the Golf Course will know where this plant is. It is easily uprooted, so is not found on exposed shores or by fast flowing waters so please don't dig it up as it is the only specimen I have found in this vicinity. The stiff upright stems are branched. The leaves are keeled and strap shaped, and the fruits are a beaked prickly green which are bur-like in appearance hence the common name. The spherical flower heads on this plant are both male and female. The female flowers are greenish and the smaller upper male flowers are yellow. Seeds are mainly dispersed by birds but growth is perpetuated by its spread of its rhizomes, a horizontal underground root system. It is seen here in the middle of the photograph growing alongside the familiar poppy.

Burnet Rose

The Burnet Rose grows on dry open places and will be
seen on the dunes all over Dunstanburgh flowering
from May to July reaching a height of 60cm. In the past
botanists called this plant Rosa spinosissima which
literally means the 'spiniest rose' and when observed this
is no mean exaggeration. It has both straight prickles and
stiff bristles. It is now known as the Rosa pimpinellifolia,
Rosa being the Latin for Rose and pimpinella meaning
twice pinnate as in the plant Salad Burnet. The Burnet
Rose is unique among the wild roses where the fruits
are rounded purplish black instead of the usual red and
scarlet hips.

Carline Thistle

A Thistle of legend. In the 8th century King Charlemagne's army became stricken with the plague so he prayed to God for a cure. The Angels came and told him to shoot an arrow and whichever plant the arrow landed on would be that cure. It landed on the Carline Thistle and was then known as Carlina, a corruption of Charlemagne's name. It is also known as the Boar's Throat, because the prickly appearance of the flower heads was thought to resemble the rough hairs around a Boar's Throat. It is found on dry grassland, quarries and cliffs, and will be recognised by its distinctive flower heads that look like a dying daisy or a thistle going to seed, but it is in full bloom. Its leaves are oblong with wavy edges. Today, preparations from the root stock are still used in proprietary medicines for digestive disorders. The plant flowers from June to October and grows to a height of 30cms.

Chickweed

As the name suggests it is a plant that is eaten by birds of all descriptions. It is unlikely that there are any pet rabbits and guinea pigs that have not been fed this succulent plant. It is also eaten by ourselves as a salad or lightly cooked. However Chickweed is a serious weed and like successful weeds it is self-pollinating and will be seen flowering most of the year. Additionally, it will be found almost anywhere. Like Stitchwort its botanical plant name is Stellaria, Latin for starry, because of the flowers resembling a star. An interesting feature of this plant is the single line of hairs on the stem which change sides at each pair of leaves. Moisture is absorbed by the hairs, the surplus trickling down the stem to the next pair of leaves where the process starts again. A magnifying glass is recommended. The plant is usually prostrate having weak stems but will clamber through its surrounding neighbours reaching 30cm. Look out for the Mouse Eared Chickweed, a hairy variety which prefers drier, disturbed grassy areas.

Cleavers or Goosegrass

It is found all over Britain in hedges, wasteland, beaches and scrub - in fact, everywhere. It is a straggling climbing plant that clings to animal's fur and our clothes by means of fine hairs with hooks which cover the four angled-stem and leaves. It has an incredible successful way of seed dispersal. Think of Velcro and this plant is it! The names given to it reflect the clinging properties of the plant. Here are a few. Clivers, Stickywilly, Stickyjack, Stickylea, Catchweed, Robin run the Hedge, Bedstraw, Scratchgrass, and Grip Grass. There are many more. Bedstraw may seem odd but it is a member of the Bedstraw family and many years ago the dried foliage used to be used to stuff mattresses. As the name implies it is a favourite food of Geese. Its botanical name is Galium

... Cleavers or Goosegrass

aparinem. Gala is Greek for milk and aparine is the Latin
for Goose. There are a number of uses for ourselves. In
the 16th century the plant's juices have been uses as a
slimming aid and as a prevention of Scurvy. The plant is
related to coffee and quinine; the roots dried and roasted
apparently make a good substitute for coffee. You can
see the plant flowering from May onwards with very
small white flowers 2 to 3 mm across, and with obliging
neighbouring foliage will be seen sprawling to heights
well in excess of 3metres.

Cow Parsley

This is the most common of the parsleys covering the hedgerows in country lanes in the early spring, with its masses of frothy white flowers in the form of large flat umbels (umbrella like clusters) and fern like leaves. When crushed these give off an aniseed scent. It has a folk lore name of 'Queen Anne's Lace' which is descriptive of its frothy appearance, but many of its other names are not so attractive. 'Devil's Meat', Bad Man's Oatmeal' and 'Adder's Meat' are a few. This is because there are many similar looking plants belonging in the Parsley family and many of them have toxic properties. Fool's Parsley and Hemlock are both poisonous and to the unwary resemble the Cow Parsley which is harmless, and is considered to be edible.

Daisy

Along with the Dandelion probably one of the most
recognisable of our wild flowers. The name Daisy comes
from the word 'day's eye' and on a sunny day can be seen
opening then facing and following the sun until sunset
when the flower will close and will wait for the next
sunny day. Folklore has given the Daisy many names.
Here are some of them: Child's Flower, Field Daisy, Little
Star, Billy Button, Measure of Love, Moon Daisy, and
Open Eye. There are dozens more. Bairnwort is another,
as the flower is considered the flower of innocence due
to its long standing tradition with children. (Remember
those Daisy Chains!). Daisy is also a nickname of girls
called Margaret after the French name Marguerite which
is the Ox Eye Daisy. Medicinal use has not escaped this
plant. Its leaves have been applied to bruises, hence

another name Bruisewort. Infusions of the flowers have been used for a variety of ailments, for example blood conditions and kidney disorders amongst others. Its scientific name is Bellis perennis both Latin names which mean pretty perennial, and this perennial owes much to its survival by its flat rosette of leaves which spread close to the ground, but too close for animals to graze and lawn mowers to cut. It flowers most of the year.

Eyebright

In the sixteenth century it was observed that its resemblance to a blood shot eye indicated that this plant was a cure for diseases of the eye. It is also called Meadow and Red Eyebright. It has a long history as a herbal treatment of the eyes and herbalists still sell extracts from this plant together with the herb Golden Seal as an eye potion. A visit to the website under  Eyebright will reveal many such potions. Euphrasia, its generic name, is a Greek word meaning to gladden. Again this is because of its reputedly medicinal power to be able to gladden the eye. The active ingredients in the plant are tannins which are thought to decrease inflammation. It is a semi-parasitic plant and is at its most successful when it attaches itself to other plants such as Clover and Plantain. It is a complex plant hybridising with one another giving rise to around fifty species in Europe, but gernarally each species is confined to its own locality. The plant is common on pastures, heaths and woods, and can be seen from June onwards growing to a height of 30cm.

Feverfew

A plant introduced from Europe centuries ago as it was held in high regard as a medicine for feminine ills. The common name of Feverfew is derived from the Latin Febrifuga meaning that the flower had the power to drive away fears. Its botanical name is Tanacetum parthenium where the former is Latin for the old plant name and the species name comes from the Greek Parthenos meaning maidens which upholds the theory that Feverfew was useful and held in high esteem for women. However, other opinions say it is a reference to the virginal white flowers. It was grown commercially as a drug but no more. It is merely regarded as an invasive weed, but is far from being an untidy plant. It is often found growing around homes against walls. July to August is its flowering time.

Garlic Mustard

It is easily recognised by the regular features distinctive of the cabbage family of four petals in the form of a cross. Also known as Jack by the Hedge, it will be found in farmyards woods and gardens, being a lover of soils rich in nutrients. It can also be recognised by the aroma of onion/garlic when the leaves and stems are crushed. It is the only member of the cabbage family to smell of garlic. Butterflies are attracted by the scent of the oils in the leaves, and this plant is a valuable food source of the Green Veined White and the Orange Tip butterflies. As expected it has, and still is, used to flavour sauces for fish and meat and in France the seeds are used to flavour food directly. The plant attains a height to 120cm flowering from April to June. The leaves survive the winter having a natural anti-freeze.

Grass of Parnassus

Growing on Mount Parnassus in Greece it was described by the Greek physician Dioscorides of the 1st century AD as a beautiful plant to grace this hill, however, cattle grazing apparently developed a taste for it. It is not a grass and does not even look like a grass but is a herbaceous dicot; grasses belong to the monocot group. Its appearance is waxy and gets its common name from the green veins which are nectar guides seen in the five white petalled flowers held aloft on single stems. The flowers smell very faintly of honey. The flowers have five stamens and a further ring of feathery stamens which distinguishes it from the Saxifrages. The leaves when boiled were once said to aid digestion and are able to disolve kidney stones. It is also known as the Bog Star as its habitat is mainly coastal in wet marshes, wet meadows and dune slacks. It will be seen flowering from July to October. This flower was taken on Holy Island, but the plant will be seen on the walk from Low Newton going north.

Greater Stitchwort

As the name suggests this plant was a remedy for the 'stitch' or any pains in the side. Its botanical name is Stellaria holostea, stellaria coming from the Latin for star (the same as the Chickweed) and the species name coming from two Greek words, 'holo' meaning whole and 'ostea' meaning bones, and as deduced was once used in healing bone fractures. It grows happily alongside the Red Campions and Bluebells and is found

in hedgerows and woodlands between April and June. Identification can be made from the flower which has five deeply divided petals, with sepals half that size and ten yellow stamens. The leaves are narrow and lance shaped arranged in opposite pairs on a square stem. As with many plants it has a folklore history. It is also known as Thunder Flower. Superstition says that if picked it will induce thunder. Other names such as Snap Jack refer to the noise the pods make when split between the fingers. It is closely related to the Chickweed and like Chickweed has been cooked as a vegetable.

Hawthorn

Hawthorn is more of a tree or shrub but worth inclusion because it is common throughout Britain. Spring sees the clusters of white flowers and in the autumn, the familiar red berries. It is also known as May, May blossom, Maythorn, Quickthorn, Whitethorn, Motherdie and Haw. It is home to over 150 species of insect species. These include the Hawthorn Shield Bug, Common Flower Bug, Earwig, Cockchafers, Bees, the Lacewing, Ladybird and many others and these in turn are meals for the Garden Spider, Wrens, Tits, and many others. The berries are a bonus for many birds including the Chaffinches, Starlings, Blackbirds, Thrushes, Robins and Yellowhammers. Hawthorn also provides hibernation shelter for small mammals, such as the Wood Mouse.

... Hawthorn

Hedge Bindweed

The white trumpet like flowers are a familiar sight in the hedgerows later in the summer. It can continue to flower well into late October. It has many names. Here are some of them: Rope Bind (because of the twisting woody stems), Hooded Bindweed, Bride's Gown, Heavenly Trumpets, White Witches Hat, Old  Man's Night Cap and Morning Glory. Morning Glory gets its name because the flower does not close up at night and the morning sun is reflected in the bloom. However it has the dubious honour of being recognised as a noxious weed. When it colonises hedges it becomes difficult to disentangle. It entwines itself around anything (anticlockwise) often crowding out other plants. Its seeds can lay dormant for up to thirty years and its creeping roots can reach up to four metres. It used to have the botanical name of Convolvulus after its ability to entwine itself, but now has the name of Calystegia sepium. The first name comes from the Greek kalyx for cup and stege for covered. Sepium is Latin for 'of hedges'. Although considered a weed it can provide excellent cover as a screen and is often seen covering old derelict buildings. It has the medical property of being a very strong purgative. Beware.

Hedge Mustard

Easily recognised by the way the flowering stems jut out at practically right angles to the main stem whilst the seed pods grow erect and hug the stem. It can grow to a height of 100cm from May to September and will be found by roads and tracks, the appearance of being rather dusty, neglected and scruffy. It has a bristly stem with small yellow flowers in the form of a cross, as with all those of the cabbage family. As the fruits ripen the flowers elongate and the seed pods hug the stem. As the name suggests it has been used in kitchens of yesteryear, usually reserved as a sauce to accompany fish dishes. In 16th century France it was recommended as an infusion to be used as a gargle to improve vocal performance.

Hogweed

It used to be fed to pigs hence its common name. The young leaves were also eaten by us and by all accounts tasting like asparagus. Its botanical name is Heracleum sphondylium. Its generic name comes from the Greek warrior Heracles, known to the Romans and us as Hercules, who used the plant medicinally. Extracts from the plant are still used today for the alleviation of bronchitis and other respiratory complaints. Its species name comes from the Latin for rounded. It is a tall plant growing well in excess of 2 metres with hollow ridged stems well remembered for being used as pea shooters. It has twenty or so branches at the top of the stem which bear the flattened flower heads called 'umbels'. Hogweed is often disregarded as just another common plant but

... Hogweed

along with its cousin the Giant Hogweed it does have a
certain grandeur. The Giant Hogweed will reach heights
up to 5 metres with leaves 2 metres long and flower
heads 50cms across. There are such grand specimens
not very far from Dunstanburgh growing by a burn. Be
aware, although the plant has been used in the kitchen,
and is not poisonous, the sap can cause blistering of the
skin. As with the majority of plants belonging to the
carrot family, of which the Hogweeds are a member, they
can cause this unpleasant condition.

Honesty

Honesty is more likely to be identified by its unique seed pods which are oval and translucent. These silvery seed pods are called silicles. These seed pods have given rise to a number of other names. In the United States it is called the Silver Dollar. It is a native of South East Asia where it is called the 'money plant'. Moonwort and Satin Flowers are other names for it. Its Generic name is Lunaria which is derived from the word Luna meaning moon. It is a garden escape and

often it will be seen well naturalised in hedgerows and woodlands, close to civilisation. It is a hairy plant with four petalled flowers which are usually purple but there is a variance of colour from white, lilac, blue to purple. It is an early flowering plant often as early as April growing up to 70cms. When the flowers are finished we are left with seed pods which are likely to be seen in dried flower arrangements. The photograph below was taken on the road leading down to Dunstanburgh Golf Club.

Knotgrass

An often overlooked plant because of the insignificance of its small white flowers. It is also prostrate and sprawling, often spreading its stems well over 2 metres along the  ground. Its botanical name is Polygonum aviculare where poly is Greek for many and gony Greek for knee. Its species name aviculare comes from the Latin for birds, as birds feed off this plant. Both the common and botanical names are references to the many swellings where the leaf joins the stem, looking like a knee with a bandage. Other names include Iron Grass, Swine's and Pig Grass. When pigs were off their food Knotgrass was the remedy to get them eating again. It is a tough and troublesome weed and can withstand trampling on paths, roadsides and paving stones where it is often found growing in the cracks. Its seeds can survive in the soil until the ground is cultivated and the seeds are brought to the surface. Medicinally it has been used as a diuretic, which helps the body get rid of excess water and salts through the passing of urine. Quaintly known as water pills. The plant flowers from June onward; look on any pathway and it will eventually be spotted.

Meadowsweet

Meadowsweet was one of the plants strewn across floors, banqueting halls and chambers to mask smells of centuries ago. The Celtic priests cherished this plant as the flowers were used to flavour mead. It was then called 'Meadwort'. The plant is aptly named as it does give off a heady smell of sweetness. It is still used in Brides' garlands and posies. The botanical name is Filipendula ulmaria, where the former word comes from the Latin filum, literally meaning hanging on a thread. Ulmaria comes from ulmus, meaning elm; the leaves are similar in appearance to those of the Elm tree. The plant contains salicylic acid that is the aspirin, which is used for a variety of ailments. The flowers can be dried to make tobacco and the roots to make flour. You can see the plant from June onwards easily reaching heights up to 150cm.

Ox-Eye Daisy

A flower which adorns roadsides, railway embankments and meadows. It has many names. Here are a few. Pretty Maids, Moon Penny, Moon Flower, Big Daisy, Bull Daisy, Herb Margaret, Dog Daisy and Horse Daisy. There are many others. The flower heads are solitary with an outer ring of white florets surrounding a central disc of golden florets, often exceeding 50mm in diameter, and the plant itself attaining a height on 1metre. Medicinally it has been used to treat wounds and a variety of ailments from liver to chest complaints. Its sap was extracted to stop runny eyes.

Ramsons

Ramsons are a wild relative of Chives. They have star shaped flowers atop triangular stems and large glossy dark green leaves. They grow in deciduous woods and shady places filling the air with that characteristic aroma of garlic. It will be seen from April onwards growing alongside Celandines and Bluebells. Other names include Bear's Garlic, Bear Leak, Wood Garlic, Broad Leaved Garlic and Buckrams. Its botanical name is Allium ursinun the first name is Greek for garlic and the latter is from the Latin ursus for bear, meaning that it was only fit for bears to eat. Apparently the Brown Bear has a taste for the bulbs and it is a favourite of the Wild Boar. It is still foraged by ourselves and eaten in salads and is said to be good for high blood pressure. Be aware if foraging, it can be mistaken with the Lily of the Valley which are poisonous, but crushing the leaves will release the recognisable scent of garlic.

Scentless Mayweed

A common plant and a member of the Daisy family found on coastal cliffs, shingle beaches, wasteland and verges. It is best recognised by its leaves which are deeply divided, with the leaf ending in a point. From a distance the whole leaf structure is a blur; no individual leaf stands out. Its botanical name is Matricaria maritima. Matricaria comes from the Latin word matrix meaning womb, as once it was used for female complaints. As with many plants growing in coastal regions its species name maritime means 'by the sea'. Although called Mayweed it does not flower in May. Too early. The connection is because the common name Mayweed comes from the Old English for maiden. Scentless Mayweed grows to a height of 60cms and flowers from July.

Scurvy Grass

It is not a grass but a member of the cabbage family. It is a recognised herb known to have anti-scorbutic qualities, that is, it has the effect of curing or preventing scurvy. As the name suggests it has been used extensively as a foodstuff to combat scurvy, a disease more synonymous with seafarers, but it used to be sold in London and elsewhere as a winter green as it is rich in vitamin C. Even to the end of the 19th century an infusion of Scurvy Grass was taken more or less the same way we have our orange juice today. The leaves apparently have a strong peppery taste similar to horseradish and watercress. It is still used in salads. The plant will be found around the coast of Britain, likely to be seen alongside the Sea Pinks and Campions. The flowers are small and white in the shape of a cross, (the Cruciferae family), and the leaves are kidney or spoon-shaped (another name: Spoonwort) that are succulent and feel waxy to the touch. Its botanical name is Cochlearia officinalis. Coch comes from the Latin for spoon shaped (the leaves) and officinalis is again Latin meaning 'of the apothecary'. So herbalists have made use of this plant for some time. Although the greenery is there all year round the plant starts flowering from May onwards.

Sea Sandwort

A plant that forms large mats of fleshy oval leaves with greenish white flowers up to 8mm in diameter. It is a great coloniser of dunes and beaches, being tolerant of salt conditions. In autumn Sea Sandwort is like a deciduous tree. It sheds its leaves then lies under the sand and waits for spring. Its botanical name is Honkenya peploides. Honkenya named after the German botanist G.A.Honkenya and the latter name pepo, Latin for pumpkin, and oides meaning that the seed pods look like pumpkins. When you see this plant it may remind you of the seed pods in the science fiction films 'Alien'. The young shoots are rich in vitamin C and have been eaten both cooked and raw, and the leaves eaten as a sauerkraut. In Iceland the plant is steeped in sour whey and allowed to ferment. The result is a liqueur likened to olive oil. Sea Sandwort is related to the Chickweed, and has been called Sea Chickweed, Seaside Sand Plant, Ovate Sandwort, and Ovate Sea Purslane. It can be seen all around this coast and will be flowering from May.

Shepherd's Purse

The name describes the flower, which show the seed pods shaped as a purse, and the seeds, if picked when ripe, will fall out as if they were coins. Its name of Capsella bursa-pastoris is the Latin for capsule, purse, and shepherd or lowly countryman. It is also known as Bad Man's Oatmeal, and Mothers

Heart, which are two strange contrasting names. A common, hardy and distinct plant that will grow just about anywhere, from cultivated soils to wasteland. In poor soils the sticky seeds are encouraged in their growth by obtaining extra nutrients from insects which become attached to them. A valuable asset indeed. It is a member of the cabbage family having four petals to form a cross, and six stamens, the white flowers in clusters on top of the stem. Medicinally the whole plant (with the exception of the roots) has been used, normally in the form of an infusion. It is said to lower the blood pressure and constrict the blood vessels, generally a good all round tonic. In the Far East it is a common food source. In Korea there is a dish called Namul with ingredients including fresh greens and wild vegetables where the roots of Shepherd's Purse are utilised. You will see the plant from March onwards growing up to 30cm.

Sneezewort

Centuries ago the root of Sneezewort held between the teeth was thought to alleviate toothache, or, particularly for that stuffy or 'bunged up' feeling from a cold. There is the remedy of powdered Sneezewort stuffed up the nose to induce sneezing which clears the head and that is where it gets its common name from. Its botanical name is Achillea ptarmica, its species name coming from the Greek ptairo, to sneeze.

The leaves are deeply cut and look feathery-like, so it shares the same plant name as the Yarrow or Milfoil, Achillea, meaning a thousand leaves. It is a wild plant but has been taken into the garden and cultivated for its attractive white blooms. The leaves have been eaten either cooked or raw, but the plant is poisonous to cattle sheep and horses. It is a plant that prefers a damp habitat, and when in flower it will attract a wide range of pollinating insects particularly hoverflies. Once established, seed reproduction becomes secondary as it has a vigorous fibrous rootstock system which spreads rooting at the nodes. Sneezewort flowers from June onwards reaching a height of 60cms.

Snowdrop

'Snow Piercer' is another name for this flower. It is a well named description of this plant as it signals that winter is on its way out. It flowers early because it stores its food in the bulb so it does not have to extract nutrients from the still frozen ground. When piercing the snow there is a spathe or protective sheath which covers the stem so protecting the flower when pushing its way through the snow. There is a single flower on each stem with two lance type leaves. When seeding the capsules split and the seeds simply drop to the ground close to the parent plant forming large colonies. Its botanical name is Galanthus rivalis, where Gala is Greek for milk, and Anthos is Greek for flower. Its species name Rivalis comes from The Latin meaning 'of snow'. Other common names

... Snowdrop

are Candlemas, Dingle Dangle and February Fairmaids.
Snowdrop is recognised as a symbol of purity and has
its associations with Candlemas Day which falls on the
2nd February, a feast celebrating the purification of the
Virgin Mary. Snowdrop is a native of Southern Europe
and was introduced from Italy centuries ago, another
example of a prolific garden escape. Medicinally the
plant has been used for digestive disorders. Snowdrop is
instantly recognisable and will be seen from late January
in woodlands, roadsides and ditches preferring wet
conditions.

Spring Beauty

Botanists call this type of plant perfoliate because the flower stems appear to be growing through the middle of the leaf. In fact, the leaves are fused in pairs. Its species name is perfoliata. Spring Beauty has its origins from the Pacific coast and was first spotted in Britain in the mid 19th century. The American Indians prized the bulbs of this plant as it was recognised to be valuable food source. Here it has been called Indian Lettuce and Miners Lettuce, the foliage being cooked and eaten like spinach. The plant flowers from May to July growing to a height of 30cm on waste, cultivated, disturbed and sandy soils.

Watercress

With its sharp flavour it is also known as 'Tang Tongue'.
Its botanical name is Nasturtium-aquaticum where
nasi-tortium is Latin for nose twisting due to its pungent
odour. Watercress is a native British vegetable and we
seem to eat more of it than anybody else. There are few
plants as rich in vitamin C and was much used to combat
scurvy and to purify the blood. It was early in the 19th
century that saw the commercial cultivation of this
plant. It is farmed where there is an abundance of fresh
water. Watercress will be seen in the ditches and streams
around Dunstanburgh, but it is advisable to leave well
alone. Plants that grow in stagnant water or in streams
that have flowed through pasture land may have picked
up the eggs of the liver-fluke, a parasite that attacks
the liver of sheep and can also find a home in ourselves.
The plant flowers from May to September, with its four
petalled white flowers as in all members of the cabbage
family.

White Campion

Similar to the Red Campion but with a rich scent
conspicuous in the evening which attracts the pollinating
moths. The White and Red Campion will often hybridise
giving rise to a whole range of pink variations. Unlike
many hybrids this particular hybrid is fertile and will
often hybridise with the parent plant. This is called back-
crossing, hence mixed populations exhibiting a variety of
pink shades. It is a fairly common plant of fertile ground,
is densely haired with five deeply notched petals, and
spear shaped leaves in opposite pairs. It flowers from
May and lasts well into late summer.

White Clover

A smaller plant than the Red Clover but apart from
the colour it is similar. Its botanical name is Trifolium
repens. The plants name is Latin meaning 'three'
(the leaves), and repens is Latin for 'creeping'. It is a
troublesome creeping plant. The stems take root as
they progress and once established takes some effort to
eradicate which gardeners will know all too well. The
rootstock is also persistent and is capable of surviving
many years. It is a valuable favourite of the bee-keeper
as it is one of the first flowers to supply nectar, around
June, after the Dandelion has run its time, although
the Dandelion does flower for a good part of the year.
White Clover has long petals which are only accessible to
long-tongued insects such as bees. When pollinated the
dead flowers remain folded over the hanging seed pods.
Occasionally one flower is left standing and is known in
some parts of the country as 'old maid'. White Clover will
be found everywhere in Britain mainly in grassy places.

White Deadnettle

Lamium album is its botanical name, both Latin words, meaning Nettle and White. It is an important food source for bees early on in the year before other nectar producing plants come into flower. It is common in road verges, grassy banks and disturbed ground. Superficially it is similar to the Stinging Nettle, without the stings, hence Dead or Blind Nettle. This likeness serves the purpose of deterring herbivores such as rabbits from eating it. Another name from the South West of England is the Adam and Eve plant. Turn the Nettle upside down and you will see under the lip of the flower black and gold stamens side by side, hence the name. The young leaves are edible, as with the stinging variety, but must be boiled. It has been used to alleviate a number of gastrointestinal problems. It has a long flowering period from May well into late Autumn.

Wood Anemone

Flowering from March it is an early Spring bloom in deciduous woods and coppices. It is an indicator of ancient woodland. Its species name comes from the Greek word nemorosa meaning 'of the woods' . Other names include Wind Flower, Thunder Flower and Smell Foxes. It is called Wind Flower beacause, although looking fragile, it can withstand quite strong winds. Pliny, that Greek writer said that it only came out when the wind blew. The name Smell Foxes may be because of its unatractive musky smell. Pheasants must like it though because they eat it. Two thirds up the stem are a ring of three leaves each divided into three-toothed segments then the single white flower with a hint of pink. It only opens in the sunshine otherwise it just droops gracefully. In bygone days the leaf juices have been made into a vinegar to treat ulcers and sores, but beware, the plant is poisonous, especially the roots.

Wood Sorrel

The clover like leaves is an easy identification tool. The leaves fold down at night looking like a tent, giving rise to other local names as Sleeping Clover and Sleeping Beauty. Not only do the leaves fold down, the flowers will droop in rainy weather and at night to protect its pollen. When the seed pods are ripe they will burst open flinging the seeds up to three metres. Other names include the Cuckoo Sorrel, as legend has it that the Cuckoo ate it to clear its throat, and the Aleluya plant as it bloomed between Easter and Pentecost when Psalms ending in Hallelujah were sung. In Wales, it has been named Fairy Bells as it summoned the wood dwelling elves out to play. Its name Oxalis acetosella is reference to the acidic taste of the leaves, similar to the Oxalic acid found in

... Wood Sorrel

the Common Sorrel though not related. The plant has thus been used in the kitchen for many years. Five hundred years ago it used to be a cultivated plant for this purpose. It has not escaped the herbalists, the leaves have astringent properties, and an infusion is supposed to be good for a hangover. Wood Sorrel grows to a height 15-20cms and is seen in deciduous woods in the spring sharing space with the Bluebells, Ramsons and Wood Anemones.

Yarrow or Milfoil

This plant has a long history as a healing herb, reflected in some of its other names. Arrowroot, Soldiers Woundwort, Nosebleed Plant, Old Man's Pepper, Devil's Plaything, Death Flower, (considered a token of death if taken into the home), Thousand Leaf, Thousand Seal and Snake Grass, There are many more. Its botanical name is Achillea millefolium and legend has it that the Greek warrior Achilles used Yarrow to heal the wounds made by iron weapons. A direct translation of its species name millefolium is 'thousand weed' which refers to the slits on each leaf giving the appearance of a thousand leaves. In the 17th century the leaves were eaten, cooked in a similar fashion to spinach. Also dried leaves were used as a herb. Yarrow flowers from June onwards and will

WHITE FLOWERS

... Yarrow or Milfoil

persist into November. The tight cluster of white flower heads (sometimes a delicate pink) making this an easy plant to identify.

Agrimony

The long flower spikes have given rise to the name of
Church Steeples, but it is more commonly known as
Cockbur, Sticklewood and Stickwort. Stickwort, so called
because of the plants unusual seeds that cling by their
hooked ends to animals and our clothing so ensuring
its seed dispersal. Agrimony comes from Argimome a
word which the Greeks used describing plants which
are healing to the eyes. The second word of its botanical
name Agramonia eupatoria refers to Mithridates
Eupator, a King who was a renowned concocter of herbal
remedies. It has been well used in the medicinal world, as
a stauncher of blood, used for kidney and liver disorders,
and even taken in wine as a preventative against snake
bites. The whole plant yields a yellow dye so it has been
utilised in the woollen industry. Agrimony flowers from
June to August and will be seen in fields, hedgerows and
road verges. The photograph shows it flowering in the
dunes of Dunstanburgh alongside the Bloody Cranesbill.

Bird's Foot Trefoil

This plant has more than seventy common names. Bacon and Eggs is probably the most well-known referring to the red streaks on the flowers. Here are some more names. Fingers and Thumbs, Lady's Fingers, Lady's Shoes and Stockings, (referring to the flower shape), Deer Vetch, Crow Toes, Cat's Clover, Devils Claw, Hop o'my Thumb, Sheep Foot, Butter and Eggs, Hen and Chickens, Yellow Trefoil, Bloom Fell, Tom Thumb, and Ground Honeysuckle. The list goes on. Its botanical name Lotus corniculatus. Lotus is Greek for the plant's name and corniculatus is the Latin for horned. It is the seed pods which resemble the Bird's Foot. The long seed pods resemble claws and give rise to another less fanciful name of Granny's Toe Nails. The Trefoil part of the name refers to the leaves, which on first sight seem to be three but in fact there are five. There are two more close to the stem. It is somewhat unusual for a plant to have so many folklore names as the plant has no recognised economic or medicinal value; however it is the food source of a number of butterflies which include the Common Blue, the Clouded Yellow, the Dingy Skipper, the Green Hairstreak and the Burnett Moths. Bumblebees are fond of leguminous plants (the Pea family such as this) and the Red- tailed bumblebee is especially fond of yellow flowers so the Bird's Foot Trefoil is a favourite. You can see the flower in bloom from May onwards growing on wasteland heaths, scrub and grassland.

Biting Stonecrop

A curious folklore name for this plant is 'Welcome home my husband however drunk you be', probably due to its long association with people. It is often seen growing on house roofs possibly guiding the drunken husband home. Other names include Wall Pepper and Goldmoss Stonecrop. It grows as a creeping ground cover mainly in a sandy environment where other plants can't get a hold. It is common enough in masonry cracks, walls, sand, shingle and similar. It is shallow rooting. The plant sits atop a rosette of succulent egg shaped leaves retaining a water supply, and has star shaped yellow flowers, with five petals, five sepals and ten stamens. Its botanical name is Sedum acre, the Latin acre means sharp, as the leaves have a sharp taste, and the sedum comes from the Latin sedo to sit. It has had uses medicinally mainly in the ailments of animals, but not so much for ourselves. You can see the plant from May to July on dry well drained land. It grows to a height of 10cms.

Black Medick

This plant can be easily confused with the Hop Trefoil but the Medick has that characteristic tiny sharp tip in the middle at each end of the leaflet which is distinguishable in the photograph. Medick has globe-like yellow flowers which can accommodate up to fifty separate florets and the fruits blacken when ripening. The seed pods do not split open to release the seeds. The seed itself forces a root out of the pod wall. Although called Medick it has nothing to do with medicine. Its botanical name is Medicago lupulina, both Latin words. The first name means Plant of the Medes which was an ancient Middle Eastern community and the species name means hop-like which refers to the Hop Trefoil, not the hop for brewing. The plant is a lover on sunny places, and will be seen on shingle beaches and dunes as well as grassland. It flowers from May growing to 50cms.

Bog Asphodel

Its botanical name is Narthecium ossiffragum. Narthecium means 'little rod' in Greek which refers to the stems and the species name comes from two Latin words meaning bone breaking or weak bone. There was an old belief that sheep that ate it developed brittle bones and recent research has upheld this legend as the Bog Asphodel does contain chemicals that have an adverse effect on bones. It is also likely that any absence of mineral salts in the soil does affect the quality of grass which the sheep feed on. The sulphur bright yellow flowers turn a deep orange at the end of their flowering season and the orange fruits have been used as a colorant to replace Saffron. Maiden Hair is another name as an extract from the yellow flowers has been used as a dye for the young maidens of Lancashire. Wet boggy places are the habitat of this plant and it can be seen in flower from June.

Bristly Ox Tongue

A stiff bristly scruffy herb that was traditionally used as an anthelmintic treatment, that is, a medication capable of causing the evacuation of parasitic worms. Its generic name Picris comes from the Greek word bitter, referring to the white sap which exudes from the stem when broken, so maybe that has something to do with it. The species name echiodes refers to the stem and leaves which are bristly. The plant can easily be mistaken for the Sow Thistle and a reliable way of identifying the Ox Tongue are the bristles on the leaves; where the bristle comes out of the leaf there is a white pimple or blister. This is shown on the leaf to the left of the flower below. The Sow Thistle does not have these pimples. However unappetising these 'blistered or pimpled' leaves may look the leaves have been cooked and eaten and by all accounts are quite edible. The plant flowers later in the year, and will be seen in rough disturbed grassland and around the coastal regions.

Broom

It is related to Gorse but much less spinier, and like Gorse a magnificent sight when in flower in the early summer. Again much like Gorse it has had an important role to play in the rural economy. It has been used for animal fodder and bedding, and of course gathered and brought together to make brooms. Food and medicine have not been excluded from its uses. An infusion of the flowers are said to be a good tonic, and the flowers have been used to make a country wine. The plant is steeped in legend, stories of love and magic as in the ballad of Broomfield Hill. Broom has given its name to towns and villages which include Brompton and Bromley. Broom will flower from early in the year, and will be seen in a variety of habitats, including shingle beaches, roadsides, river banks, heaths and cliffs, a tall shrubby plant growing in excess of 3 metres.

Cat's Ear

The common name of Cat's Ear has been given to the
small bracts on the stem which are thought to resemble
the ears of cats. Its botanical name is Hypochoeris
radicata. Hypo is Greek for below and choiros means pig
Radicata is Latin for having roots which indicates that
the leaves rise direct from the roots. Pigs are thought
to enjoy the roots of this plant as a food source hence
its generic name. It is similar to the Dandelion with its
basal rosette of leaves but the stems are branched, solid
and hairy, and they do have those bracts. Its uses are
limited but all parts of the plant are edible, especially the
young leaves, either raw or cooked. The roots, as with the
Dandelion, can be roasted and ground to form a coffee
substitute. You can see the plant flowering from June
onwards attaining a height up to 70cms.

Coltsfoot

An unusual
feature of the
Coltsfoot are the
flowers appearing
before the leaves.
So an apt folklore
name for the
Coltsfoot is 'Son
before Father'.
The yellow
dandelion-like
flowers will be
seen pushing

their way through the last of the snow. The plant
certainly likes bleak conditions where it would seem that
nothing else would grow. Other names are Tush Plant,
Foal's Foot, Foalswort, Housefoot, Ass's Foot, Coughwort,
Farfara, Horse Hoof, and Bull Foot. It is the shape of
the leaves which give Coltsfoot its common name. The
Coltsfoot has had an important place in history as it has
been used in the kitchen and medicinally since ancient
times. Its scientific name is Tussilago farfara where
tussilago comes from the Greek; tussis meaning cough.
The leaves were dried and smoked in a pipe supposedly
for a cure for asthma, and the juices from the leaves were
regarded as a cure for a coughs, colds, burns, and an
array of minor ailments. Down from the leaves and seed
heads were used to stuff pillows and the young flowers
and buds can provide an aromatic tasty addition in
salads. You can see the plant from February.

Common Toadflax

Similar in appearance to the Snapdragon this flower can be found in meadows, cultivated fields, waste ground, and quite often growing against factory walls. Its common name has two meanings. Toad means that the plant was considered so useless it was only fit for toads, and flax because the leaves are very narrow and are spirally arranged up the stem similar to flax. Its scientific name means the same. It is Linaria vulgaris, the first word is Latin for flax and vulgaris means common, that is, worthless as in toad or dog. However, it is a fairly tall plant with bright two tone yellow flowers with an orange splash in the middle and it brightens up any waste land. The unusual shape of the flowers has given rise to dozens of folk lore names. Here is a selection. Devil's Head

... Common Toadflax

(that elongated spur), Weasel Snout, Squeeze Jaw, Pig's
Chops, Dragon Bushes, Devil's Flax and Lion's Mouth,
all referring to the way the flower opens when the sides
are squeezed. Access to the petal tube is closed by a fold
called the palate and only the insects which are heavy
enough can open up the pollen tube when landing on this
platform. Bees are such insects but they sometimes cheat
by biting the underside and stealing the pollen and in so
doing pollination will not occur. This 'biting' is a similar
practice that bees do to the Bladder Campion. It has not
found much use in the herbalist world but unsurprisingly
has been used to treat both diarrhoea, constipation,
jaundice, dropsy, haemorrhoids and cystitis. It has even
been put in chicken's drinking water to perk them up.
Toadflax can be seen flowering from June.

Cowslip

Legend says that St. Peter dropped the keys to heaven somewhere in Northern Europe and from that spot the first Cowslip grew. The nodding bunch of flowers are said to resemble a bunch of keys and that is its name in the South West of England. It has dozens of folklore names. Here are some of them. Herb Peter, Fairy Cup, Paigle, Palsywort, Key Flower, Buckles, Crewel, Petty Mulleins, and Cow Shiplings Its old English name is Cuslyppe meaning cow patti or cow dung so named because it was found in or around cow pastures. Its botanical name is Primula veris, both words from the Latin meaning first spring and it is indeed one of the first of the spring flowers. It prefers open ground and sunshine and does not thrive in woodlands or where it is crowded out by taller plants. It has had wide medicinal use - as an expectorant, rheumatic and gout complaints, coughs colds and flu, catarrh, insomnia and many more. In the kitchen the leaves and flowers have been made into puddings and wines. This is one of the plants whose seeds are included in seed mixes and used to landscape motorway banks and other civil engineering earthworks. The counties of Northampton, Surrey and Worcester, have voted it as their county flower. The cowslip grows up to 30cms and is seen from March to May.

Creeping Buttercup

Ranunculus repens is its name. Rana the Latin for frog (damp places), and repens means creeping. It can be distinguished from the other Buttercups by the way it spreads with those creeping runners which root every few centimetres so forming huge colonies. It is considered a pest by both farmers and gardeners as eradication is difficult.

Like the Creeping Thistle unless all the root parts are cleared, it will quickly regrow from a mere fragment of root. Ploughing merely breaks up the root. It is often found in meadows where the cattle will not eat it. It is slightly poisonous and does have an unpleasant taste. The grass around the Buttercup is grazed, but the Buttercup remains uneaten which allows it to spread even further. Along with the Meadow and Bulbous Buttercup there has been the old-age tradition of children holding a Buttercup under the chin and if there is a reflection that person likes butter. It has been used as an ointment for skin problems, bruises, bites and sores. It once had the name of 'crazies' because the smell was supposed to cause insanity. Although it is a nuisance weed the Buttercups, and especially the tall majestic Meadow Buttercup, make a showy sight of bright yellow from May to October.

Dandelion

The leaves give Dandelion its name. The resemblance of the sharp pointed lobes of the leaves leads to a corruption of the French words 'dent de lion', or Lion's tooth. Other intriguing names include Pissabed, Devil's Milk Pail and Heart Fever Grass. It is one of the most abundant of the common weeds in Britain with over 300 sub species and there are botanists who make the study of the Dandelion their sole subject. The plant is thought to have evolved some 30 million years ago in Eurasia and has been used by humans as a food source and herb for as long as history has been recorded. Its botanical name is Taraxacum officinalis. The plant's name comes from the Latin meaning a Persian bitter herb, and its species name of officinalis is a reference to a Monastic herb

... Dandelion

store. The leaves can be cooked or eaten raw as a salad; the roots can be dried, roasted and ground to make a caffeine free Dandelion coffee. One of the ingredients of root beer is the root of this plant, and who can forget the drink Dandelion and Burdock. The flower heads are used to make country wine and in the television programme 'River Cottage Garden' jam was made out of the flower heads. The Dandelion has not escaped being used as a medicine. It has had its uses clearing up a variety of complaints from jaundice to consumption. For the many years this plant has been of service to mankind it is still much maligned, but it is unlikely to lose too much favour with the generations of children telling the time by counting the number of puffs it takes to blow away the parachute seeds, unwittingly helping the plant to colonise elsewhere. It will be seen in abundance from April onwards.

Evening Primrose

This plant is a native of the Americas but is now naturalised in Europe and encroaches into the Southern hemisphere. Its botanical name is Oenothera biennis, which is not very exciting as the plant is a valued commodity and is used extensively in the medicinal world. Its generic name is the Greek name for the flower, and the species name is Latin for biennial. As the common name suggests the flower blooms in the evening when it is pollinated by night flying moths. The well-known Primrose Oil, which is to be seen in all pharmaceutical outlets is extracted from the seeds and contains an essential fatty acid called Gammalinolenic Acid and is considered necessary for body development and growth. It has been used since the 1930's as a

... Evening Primrose

traditional remedy for eczema, but has also been used
to alleviate women's complaints, the treatment of high
blood pressure, a cure for baldness, and even a treatment
for laziness. Not unsurprisingly it has been a food source
to us, the roots boiled as potatoes, but the leaves must
not be consumed. This particular specimen was taken
on Holy Island close to the Marsh Helleborines and the
Buglosses, and is likely to be a garden escape. In the
Southern Counties it is widespread and will be seen in
road verges. Also known as Sun Caps and Sun Drops it
will be seen flowering from May growing up to 1500cms
in height.

Fleabane

A native plant of Europe and Asia it will be seen on marshy ground, by rivers and ditches. As the common name suggests it was once the scourge of fleas. Fleabane when dried and burned gave off a vapour that drove fleas away. When, in its natural state strewn along the floors of homes those many centuries ago, seemed to act as an insecticide where the fleas were attracted to the plant's aroma, succumbed to the smell and died. Nicholas Culpeper, the 17th century herbalist said that the fleas lived the plant so much they never left 'till they met their death! Its botanical name is Pulicaria dysenterica. Its generic name comes from the Latin pulex for flea, and its species name as you might have guessed, is a reference to the times when its use medicinally was as a cure for dysentery. A potion of the crushed foliage was also used as a soothing balm for cuts, sores and bruises. It is a member of the Daisy family, its seed dispersal is similar, and although rarer in the Northern Counties of England can be seen from July onwards.

Goat's Beard

Another common name is Jack-Go-To-Bed-At-Noon on account of the flowers opening very early in the morning and closing around noon. Its name of Tragopogon pratensis comes from the Greek pogon meaning beard and the species name is Latin for of meadows. Goat's Beard is named after the tufts of silky hairs surmounting the fruit. The plant looks very much like a Dandelion but is considerably bigger and when not in flower it will be recognised by the long narrow leaves arising from a solid stem, somewhat grass like in appearance. The fruiting head is also much like the Dandelion's familiar 'clock', but much larger in size. In days gone by the long tap roots were dug up and cooked as parsnips and boiled in milk. It was considered to be as good a tonic as anything after an illness. It grows up to 70cms in a variety of habitats including grassland, dunes and roadsides and will be seen in flower from June to July.

Gorse

There is an old saying 'when Gorse is out of bloom, kissing's out of season'. On warm days the air is filled with that coconut fragrance, and on hot days the ripened pods can be heard cracking open and releasing their seeds. It has had its uses in the past as fuel (once it was a mainstay of rural economy and Gorse has the ability to regenerate quickly), thatching, fodder for farm animals, hedging, and the corralling of livestock because it is so thorny. Not escaping its usage as a medicine, it has been used to treat jaundice and urinary complaints. Furze and Whin are other names for Gorse, especially Whin in the North of England. Its botanical name is Ulex europaeus. Ulex is the Latin name given by Pliny, the Roman Author, Naturalist and Philosopher of some two thousand years ago. Europaeus means of Europe but there is an old Anglo Saxon name of 'Gorst' meaning wasteland. Very apt.

Groundsel

Its botanical name is Senecio vulgaris. The plant name of Senecio is Latin for Old man referring to the seeding flower heads which resemble shaving brushes. The vulgaris part of the name means common and it certainly is. Besides being known as Old Man in the spring, it has other names. Birdseed,  Simson and Squaw Head are some. This plant is a prolific coloniser. It can germinate and seed within a matter of weeks so will flower practically throughout the year and along with Chickweed is one of the first arrivals in January. Its seed dispersal is like that of the Dandelion and is very successful. This gives rise to its Anglo Saxon name of Grondesweyle meaning ground swallower. In Northern England and Scotland it is sometimes known as Grundyswallow or Ground Glutton. In the 17th century it was used as a poulticing herb for sore skin and was supposed to cure the horse ailment called 'staggers', so has been used medicinally but be aware, the plant is poisonous to humans. You will see the plant growing almost anywhere up to a height of 30cm.

Herb Bennet

A plant which is steeped in folklore mystique. It has had a long association with Christianity and would appear that the magical power this flower has its connections with St.Benedict, the founder of that particular order of monks. In the region of 500 years ago it was considered one of the most powerful charms to see off any evil spirits. Hung over doors it would stop the devil from entering the home. Early medical writings said that if the root of this plant was carried about the person no venomous beast could harm him. Its botanical name is Geum urbanum, geum is Latin but comes from the Greek geno meaning fragrant, and its species name is from the Latin meaning 'relating to towns' which is why it is often found next to buildings and old stone walls. The

... Herb Bennet

roots have a clove like aroma and were used as both a
fly repellent and for flavouring ales and the Benedictine
liqueurs. Medicinally, infusions were taken to help with
stomach upsets, and apparently when added to bathwater
is a cure for cuts and piles. Herbalists still use the plant
today but there is little scientific evidence to substantiate
these claims. The plant is also known as Clove Root, Herb
of St.Benedict, Goldy Star and Wood Avens. It is related to
the Water Aven which is found in ditches and wet ground
and when growing in proximity will cross pollinate. Herb
Bennet grows to a height of 60cms and will be seen in
flower from June.

Kidney Vetch

As might be expected from its English name it was expected to cure kidney complaints, this belief coming from the flower heads which are kidney shaped. It has other names. Here are a few. Butter Fingers, Lady's Slipper, Lady's Finger's, Crow Nose, Lamb's Foot and Pincushion. Each flower has its own hairy calyx which contains the sepals  giving the flower that woolly appearance. Its scientific name is Anthyllis vulneraria. The first word is Latin for the plant's name and the species name is Latin for wound healer. Besides its once valued remedy for kidneys, a mild infusion was used to wash wounds and drank as a tonic. It was supposed to stop children vomiting. The plant is a rich source of nectar but only the stronger insects can prise out the petal tubes. It is the Small Blue butterfly which lays its eggs on the plant which is its main food source for its young. The plant has many sub-species and there are many colour variants from pink to lemon yellow. Its preferred habitat is dry grassland by the sea and this particular photograph was taken on Holy Island in June where there are acres of them.

Lady's Bedstraw

A plant that is found in most habitats but likes well drained soils and will be seen from May to September on the dunes of Dunstanburgh with its bright frothy yellow flowers. Hay made from this plant was once used to stuff mattresses. The plant is honey scented (the Coumarin scent)  and is thought to be a natural deterrent to insects and fleas. It is also associated with the Virgin Mary. Legend has it that she had lain on a bed of this plant during the birth of Christ. In some parts of the country it is known as Cheese Rennet and has been used as a substitute to curdle cheese. A yellow dye extracted from the plant has been used by young women to dye their hair so it is also known as Maids Hair. The decoction, the extraction of the plant's essence, has been used medicinally to help a variety of complaints including urinary diseases, headaches, nosebleeds and epilepsy. The list is long. As with many plants it is a food source and one moth which is particularly partial to Lady's Bedstraw is the Hummingbird Hawk Moth.

Leopard's Bane

Its common name is from the folklore myth that this plant could kill wild beasts, when used as a poison, being added to raw meat to bate the Leopard. In late Spring Leopard's Bane will come into bloom with its bright yellow daisy like flowers. There is a single flower on each stem with heart shaped leaves which clasp the stem. It was introduced to Britain in medieval times as a medicinal herb but is now classed as a garden escape.

Lesser Celandine

Celandine is Greek for swallow, as it was thought that these birds fed their chicks this flower to improve their eyesight. Its botanical name is Ranunculus ficara, both Latin words, the former meaning Frog, that is, the plant is found in wet places, and the latter from 'ficus' relating to its fig shaped tubers. As one of the first of the wild flowers to appear on the landscape it has given rise to many folk names. The Welsh name is Llygad Ebril meaning April's Eye but can be seen blooming much earlier than this. The Gaelic name of Grianne means the sun. Pilewort is an older name and as you might have guessed has been used to treat haemorrhoids. The roots are likened to this complaint and as with many plants, the names and the shape of various parts are reflected in the name. Orchid is an example. Look that one up. The German vernacular is Scharbockskraut which means Scurvyherb. The young leaves can be eaten but as with members of the Buttercup family it contains a volatile yellow oil. It is called Protoanemonine and can cause intense oral and gastric irritation. Leave well alone! William Wordsworth was fond of the Celandine and penned many an ode in praise. There is a carving of the Celandine on his tombstone in Grasmere but it is the Greater Celandine which is odd because the two plants do not belong to the same family. The Greater belongs to the Poppy family and the lesser to the Buttercup's. This bright yellow flower is common all over Britain, a lover of damp shady places and will flower as early as March.

Marsh Marigold

This attractive plant can be described as a large Buttercup. It is found in water, fens, marshes, wet woods and so on. Its outstandingly bright yellow flowers, the blooms often attaining a diameter up to 50mm. These flowers are held on hollow stems, with the whole plant growing up to 60cm. Its botanical name is Caltha palustris. The Latin name Caltha  comes from the Greek for goblet so another popular name of King Cup is quite common. The species name of palustris is the Latin for 'of the marsh'. The plant is steeped in folklore and has a variety of names usually named where it is geographically located. Names such as Water Blobs, Pollyblobs, May Blobs, Water Bubbles, Balfe (in Caithness), and Mary Gold are often used. On Mayday, in bygone days it used to be hung over byre doors to increase the fertility of the animals and as a protection against witches and other evil spirits. It used to be used as a vegetable. The buds were used as a substitute for capers and the leaves were eaten as spring greens. The flowers had the oils extracted and were used for dying yarn. The plant will be seen flowering from April.

Meadow Vetchling

A common plant of grassy places and is found throughout Britain. It has a creeping rootstock which results in it often forming quite large clumps in the grass. It is a climbing plant and has a tendril on each leaf but this is fairly weak and it is supplemented by many square stems which rely on each other and the surrounding plants for their support. Each stem supports five to twelve flowers. It is a member of the Pea family. Its botanical name is Lathyrus pratensis, the former word is Greek for pea, and the species name is Latin for meadow. Other folklore names are Old Granny's Slipper-Sloppers and Tare tine. Tare is an old name for vetch. This vetchling is a valuable fodder plant and like others of the Legume family has nitrogen fixation properties, as the Red Clover. See the Red Clover for an explanation of this process. The plant may well exceed 120cms in height and flowers from June.

Monkeyflower

Here is a flower that was introduced into this country
early in the 19th century from the Islands off Alaska.
There it rains most of the year and it has so evolved that
it loves water and it found that the canals of Britain were
a fine way to spread and is now naturalised over most of
the U.K. Its botanical name is Mimulus guttatus, mimulus
coming from the Latin meaning little actor, and the
species name, also Latin, means spotted, referring to the
spots which are found in the flower. They can be seen in
the photograph below. Its common name is taken from
the petals which are thought to resemble the grinning
face of a monkey. The whole plant is edible, but reports
affirm that it is very salty, and medicinally, the juices
from the foliage when crushed are a soothing balm for
bruises and sores. You will see the plant in flower from
July growing to a height of 50cms.

Nipplewort

The common name comes from the vague notion that the buds have that same similarity to nipples. This plant is an example of what is called a herbal remedy, being based on the 'doctrine of signatures' where people looked for a similarity between a plant and a part of the body they wished to cure. This led to the assumption that this plant would cure ulcerated and sore nipples and apothecaries, the chemists of old, used to prescribe this plant for such complaints. These apothecaries used to call the plant 'papillaris' which comes from the Latin word papilla for 'teat'. This has been its prime medical use, however, not all plants were used with such an illogical unscientific base. It has been used as a food source as a salad plant. It is a relative of the Dandelion family but with much smaller flowers, held on many branched wiry stems, which are hollow but do not have that milky sap so familiar with the Dandelion and other plants belonging to the Daisy family. It grows up to 1metre and will be seen flowering from June.

Primrose

The plants generic name Primula comes from the Latin 'prima rosa', meaning first rose. It is not a rose but a member of the primula family, but is so called as it is one of the first flowers to herald the return of spring. This plant, like the Cowslips, produces male and female flowers and

attempts to transplant them usually fail. Due to this over collection and to restrict excessive damage to this species, picking and removal is illegal both here in the U.K. and in other countries. In the U.K. it is protected by the Wildlife and Countryside Act of 1981. Perhaps this is just as well because most of the plant is edible. The flowers have been used to make Primrose wine and the leaves for making tea. Primroses and many of the Primula family have two different flower heads which look almost identical. They are produced on different plants and are called the Pin Eyed and Thrum Eyed Primroses. Insects are not particularly abundant in early spring to carry out their pollination functions, it is mainly the ants that unwittingly do this task as they favour the seeds as a food source so spreading the seeds perpetuating growth. See the Primrose from March to May.

Ragwort

Other names include Ragweed, Stinking Willie, St. James Wort and Mare's Fart. The latter name possibly derives from having been used in infusions to cure the disease called staggers, an infection of the spinal cord and brain of domestic animals. Its botanical name is Senecio jacobaea, both Latin.

Senex means 'old man' and the species name relates to St. James, the patron Saint of Horses. The Latin name of 'senex' is the same as the Groundsel meaning 'old man', a reference to the fine white hairs when the plant is seeding. The plant is no friend of the livestock farmer. Along with the Buttercup, the Ragwort is left standing, uneaten as animals instinctively avoid it as the plant has poisonous alkaloids which can destroy the liver over a period of time. This poison is retained and remains active so is still volatile if harvested as hay. The Weeds Act defines five injurious weeds of which the Ragwort is one. The others are the Creeping and Spear Thistles and the Curled and Broad Leaved Docks. However, it has one friend, the attractive orange and black striped Cinnabar Caterpillar which enjoys this plant as a food source. Ragwort grows up to 120 cms and is a common sight of waste places, fields and roadsides from June onwards.

Rock Rose

Also known as Sun Flower and Sun Rose, it is a low growing creeping plant that likes sunny south facing rocks and cliffs. It is common throughout Dunstanburgh, identification being made by the bright yellow five petalled crinkly flowers, and dense white hairs on the underside of the leaves. Although it is called a rose it is not a member of the rose family, nor does it smell or look like one. Its name of Helianthemum nummularium means sunflower, helios being Greek for sun and anthemum Greek for flower. The species name means creeping shrub. Rock Rose only opens in sunlight. In dull and wet weather it closes its petals. The plant flowers from May onwards.

Rough Hawkbit

There are many yellow flowered members of the composite family with its many sub-species. This makes them difficult to identify. This is best left to the experts who are likely to use the leaves as a means of naming a particular species. Three members of the Daisy family which can be easily identified are the Hawkbit as shown below, the Dandelion and the Cat's Ear. These can be  distiguished from the rest by having no leaves on the flowering stem. Dandelions have a hollow stem with its white sap. The Cat's Ears have scales up the stem which resemble Cat's Ears which is how it gets common name and the Rough Hawkbit has a hairy stem with a slight swelling at the top. The Hawkbit's yellow flowers also have a reddish tinge to the underside of the petals. All these plants have a basal rosette. Its botanical name is Leontodon hispidus. The plants name comes from the Greek 'leon' meaning lion, and 'todon' meaning tooth, hence lions teeth referriong to the leaves. Its species name is Latin meaning 'with coarse bristles'. See the Hawkbits flowering from June to September reaching a height of 50cms.

Silverweed

A plant of waste places, dunes and roadsides. The Silverweed will be easily identified by its leaves. The underside is covered in silver hairs which give the appearance of the leaves shining. The flowers have five petals and are bourne on single stalks with each stalk growing out

of the leaf axils. It is a creeping plant which, like the strawberry, produces rooting stolons. Its botanical name is Potentilla anserina both Latin words meaning powerful and 'relating to Geese'. Another name for the plant is Goose Tansy so it must be assumed that Geese must have a liking for the Silverweed. Before the introduction of the potato the roots of the Silverweed were an important food source. They were boiled, ground and made into a porridge or bread, tasting like parsnips. In Somerset Silverweed is known as Bread and Cheese. It has been used in a number of propriety medicines, having much the same properties as the Creeping Cinquefoil. When steeped in milk it was supposed to remove freckles. Silverweed will flower from May to late summer.

Smooth Sow Thistle

Also known as Hare's Lettuce, Rabbit's Meat, Swine Thistle, and Dog's Thistle. There are many more names. Here is a plant that has been consumed by both animals and humans. The 'Sow' in the name refers to the juice in the stems that Sows  instinctively knew was beneficial to their milk yield after giving birth to a litter of piglets. As the folklore names indicate the Sow Thistle has been used as a fodder for rabbits and hares; ground left bare by rabbits and human activity offers favourable conditions for the plant to colonise. Identification between the Smooth and Prickly Sow Thistle can be seen by the leaves. The Smooth Sow Thistle has projections on the leaves which appear to clasp the stem, whilst the Prickly variety has ear shaped lobes which surround the stem. Its botanical name is Sonchus oleraceous, the former word being Greek for the plant, and the species name is Latin for a kitchen pot herb. It is still eaten as a salad plant, or cooked like spinach, and in France it is fed to the edible escargot (snails) in readiness for the table. The whole plant with exception of the roots is said to be a good general tonic. An infusion in the form of a tea, apparently lowers the blood pressure and constricts the blood vessels. The plant flowers from June and will attain a height of 1.5mts.

YELLOW FLOWERS

Tormentil

Tormentil has a long folklore history. Its common name comes from the Latin tormentum meaning torture when it was used to relieve the tortures of toothache. Not only toothache but mouth ulcers, and intestinal discomforts such as colic. It is a strongly astringent plant. Its botanical name

is Potentilla erecta, both Latin words. Potens meaning powerful because of its qualities as a medicine, and erecta meaning 'upright' relating to the stems. A local name for Tormentil is 'Blood Root' because it has been used as a red dye when extracted from the roots and because of its high astringent qualities has been used for tanning as an alternative to Oak bark. It is a plant characteristic of acid soils which grows on heaths, fens and bogs having four buttercup-like yellow petals, four sepals and numerous stamens. The upper leaves have three leaflets and two stipules which appear to clasp the stem. It has a close relative in the Creeping Tormentil, similar, but normally only having five petals. The plant is seen here growing amongst the heathers of Dunstanburgh, flowering from May onwards.

Welsh Poppy

This is not a Poppy of Welsh origin. It grows in most of Europe, Spain, Portugal, and France and so on, but it was first identified in Wales by the Swedish botanist Linnaeus. Its botanical name is Meconopsis cambrica, the first name is Greek for 'looking like a poppy' and the species name is Latin for Welsh. It does differ from the Opium and Common Poppy because the seeds are  released through slits on the side of the seed pod and not through the familiar pepper pot type of seed capsule. It would appear that this plant is a garden escape, but not so, it is the other way round. It is wild; gardeners liked it and cultivated it as a garden flower. Invariably it is seen in walls and cracks around houses, and is well adapted to growing in these places, since it has a plentiful supply of tiny black seeds produced at the summer's end. The only other yellow flowered poppies are the Yellow Horned Poppy which grows on the sea shore, the Californian Poppy, and the Greater Celandine. The plant will be seen in flower from April to August.

Yellow Archangel

Sometimes called the Yellow Deadnettle, it is an invasive plant of ancient woodland and hedgerows. It belongs to the same family as the dead nettles having hairy square stems with leaves in opposite pairs, alternating at ninety degrees above or below the stem. The plant flowers when the Bluebells are fading, around April time, and will be recognised by its yellow hooded flowers and the 'tongues' having red honey guides. Its name of Lamiastrum galeobdolon comes from the Latin Lamium, that is, the Deadnettle, and gale which is Greek for Weasel and obdolon meaning nasty smell. Another name for the plant is Weasel Snout. The plant does have an unpleasant smell. It may also have got its name of Archangel because it does not sting although a member of the nettle family. Alternatively, legend has it that it is a guardian of cattle against a black magic disease called elf-shot. It has been used as a cure for sores and ulcers but unusually has little herbal or medicinal use.

Yellow Flag

Also known as Yellow Iris this plant has been grown worldwide as an ornamental feature. Iris is the Greek word for rainbow, since there are variations of the colour of violet, but the flower is mainly seen with its familiar white and yellow hue. The name flag comes from the fluttering of the flowers said to resemble flags.  It is tolerant to submersion, and is invasive and tough to remove. It spreads by creeping rhizomes and water dispersed seeds. It has also been used for water treatment as it has the ability to absorb heavy metals through its roots. The rhizome has been used as a herbal remedy to treat diarrhoea, dropsy, coughs and convulsions, and a piece of the rhizome on a sore tooth is said to work wonders to relieve the pain. Red dye can be extracted from the flowers, green from the leaves, and a black dye from the roots. The sword like leaves, (Sword Flag, and Segg, which is an old Anglo Saxon word for a short sword, are other names), have been and maybe still are used for a thatching material. A tall plant, it flowers from June and cannot be overlooked at Dunstanburgh.

Yellow Rattle

The common name of Yellow Rattle is so called because of the sound produced by the ripe seeds rattling around inside their seed pods. Found mainly in meadows, a walk through a field of these plants and you will hear just that sound. Other names unsurprisingly, are Hay Shackle, Hay
Rattle, Rattlebasket and Rattlebox. Cockscomb is another in reference to the leaf. Its generic name is Rhinanthus which comes from two Greek words meaning flower and nose which in folklore is a reference to the petal tube which is likened to a witch's nose. It is a hemi-parasitic plant, that is, it obtains some of its nutrients from the roots of its neighbouring plants. In the past this was seen as a nuisance as it could reduce the hay yield as much as 50%. However on the flip side, in a garden context, this grass reduction can be made to favour the gardener by restricting grass growth, and is now often used to turn grassland back to meadows by letting the plant feed off vigorous grasses allowing others to thrive. The plant flowers from May to August and can be recognised by its spotted stem and by the petal tube having two rounded dark 'teeth', as shown here in the photograph.

Bistort

Its scientific name is Polygonum bistorta. This plant gets its name from the Latin Bistorta. Bis meaning twice and Torta meaning twisted, which is a reference to the twisted shape of its underground stems. Other names include Easter Ledges, Passion Dock, Snakeweed and Adderwort. The latter two names refer to the coiled like roots which also suggests a cure for snake bites. The root is rich in tannin and has been used for tanning leather, but is best known for being one of the most powerful astringent medicines in the vegetable kingdom. It has a proven excellence in the complaints of diarrhoea, dysentery, cholera and many bowel complaints. In the Lake District puddings are made out of the young leaves. The puddings are known as Easter-Ledge. The reason for this is to purge the body after a long winter of salted meats. You will see the plant flowering from June to September.

Common Centaury

It is a member of the Gentian family. This plant will be
found in dry grassy places, sand dunes and heaths. It is
shown here growing with the Piri Piri plant. Now there
is a clue where this specimen is. It is a variable species
that many botanists classify them into many sub-species.
It varies in size anywhere from 10 to 40cms and will
bloom from June to September. The flowers are pink and
tubular and like all flowers of the Gentian family close
in the afternoon. The stem is square and the leaves form
opposite pairs up the stem. The plants name Centaurium
erythraea is Greek for centaur. This creature, half horse
half man, supposedly used this plant to cure himself of a
wound inflicted upon himself by the nine headed serpent
Hydra. Medicinally it has been used as a remedy for all
sorts of ailments ranging from anaemia to hiatus hernia
and Nicholas Culpeper, the 17th century astrologer and
herbalist, even recommended it for removing freckles.

Common Mallow

A characteristic of this plant are the fruits which look like round cheese segments so it has other folklore names as Cheese Flower and Pancake Plant. Its botanical name of Malva sylvestris is not so interesting, both Latin words, the former being the plants name and the latter meaning woodland. As with all Mallows this is an old food plant eaten as a vegetable since Roman times. It has also been used in herbal medicine to alleviate stings and inflammation and the whole plant has a sticky glutinous sap which has been used in soothing ointments. The naturalist Pliny said that this sap mixed with water would give him day long protection against aches and pains. The sap of its cousin the Marsh Mallow is still used today in the pharmaceutical and confectionary trade. The Common Mallow will be seen from June onwards on roadsides and hedges reaching a height of 90cms.

Lady's Smock or Cuckoo Flower

Named the Cuckoo Flower as it was supposed to flower upon the first sound of the Cuckoo. Other names include Pigeon's Eye, Lucy Locket, Bittercress, Milk Maids and Fairy Flower. It is an attractive delicate flower and steeped in legend, though not very enchanting. In France if picked on May Day you would get bitten by an Adder, and in Germany, if picked by your house it would be struck by lightning. Because of these associations it is probable that little use has been made of this plant medicinally although its Latin name of Cardamine comes from the Greek kardia meaning heart. It can be eaten as a salad plant but as one of its names suggests it must be quite bitter. This plant is often covered in Cuckoo spit, but it does not get its name from this. This white froth that is exuded from the nymph of the Froghopper is to conceal themselves from predators. The plant needs a reliable source of water and will be seen round most ponds and wet habitats, flowering from April to July.

Opium Poppy

A plant that has a somewhat infamous reputation. It is usually grown as an ornamental garden flower but, as with so many plants it does escape and is recognised as one of the numerous garden escapes. This one might be called an up market

weed. Its botanical name is Papaver somniferum which is Latin for 'sleep bringing poppy', referring to the sedative properties of these plants. The use of the Opium Poppy predates written history. Images of this plant have been found on ancient artefacts around 4000BC. The sap was named by the ancient Greeks 'opion' from where it gets its modern name opium. It is the source of many narcotics including morphine (morphine is named after Morpheus, the God of sleep), its derivative Heroin, codeine, papavarine, thebaine and others. It is also a food source. Both the seeds and the oils are widely used throughout the world having low levels of opiates. Various countries of the world have differing attitudes towards the cultivation of this plant. Simplistically here in the U.K. it is legal to grow but extraction of the narcotics for refinement is illegal. You can see the plant mainly in dry habitats from June to September.

Sea Rocket

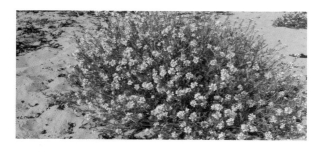

A succulent low growing plant of the sea shore, usually growing on the unattractive drift line where it is often found with the Saltworts and the Oraches. The flowers are either pink or white with four petals in that typical crucifer arrangement common of the cabbage family. It has a long tap root which finds every drop of fresh water it can and is then stored in those fleshy leaves. The root itself branches to stabilise the sand and the whole plant is often covered in sand forming their own small sand dunes. It is one of the few plants that can tolerate total submersion in salt water albeit for relatively short periods only. It has ant-scorbutic properties hence it is rich in vitamin C and useful for keeping scurvy at bay. It is said to have been used for post-malarial sickness. The young leaves can be eaten as a salad but are considered bitter. Other names include Red Bunny and Purple Sea Rocket. Its botanical name is Cakile maritima. The plants name is Arabic, since the plant is found in the deserts of Arabia. The species name is Latin for seaside. From June to August this plant grows to a height of 30cms.

Bloody Cranesbill

The plant belongs to the Geranium family. The name Geranium comes from the classical Greek Geranos meaning crane. Its botanical name is Geranium sanguineum and the latter name comes from the Latin for bloody referring to its flowers. There are a number of cranesbills so named because of their pointed fruits resembling the bird's beak – the Crane, and the Bloody Cranesbill is no exception. The Bloody Cranesbill gives a splendid show during the summer growing profusely over the dunes of Dunstanburgh, distinctive with its reddish purplish solitary flowers which are up to 35mm across held aloft on long stalks. It is not a particularly common plant but, in localised areas, can cover a lot of ground. You can see the plant from June onwards.

Common Sorrel

In late summer the Sorrel gives that bright red colouring to open grassland when the leaves, stems and flowers give that vivid crimson hue. It is a plant that has been used in the kitchen for centuries and probably still is. It would be a safe bet that the River Cottage Garden forage for it for use in their restaurant. Sorrel leaves have a distinct sourness and this flavouring was used in much the same way as lemons today. Its botanical name is Rumex acetosa, both Latin words, Rumex being the plants name and acetosa meaning acidic leaves. Rumex comes from the Latin rumo, meaning to suck, as the Romans used to suck the leaves as a means of quenching the thirst. Besides its culinary use for sauces and flavourings, it has also been used to remove ink and iron stains from linen due to the presence of its oxalic acid. The Sorrel is variable in its hybrid forms and it takes an expert to identify. Its cousin called the Sheep's Sorrel is also a familiar sight and familiar in appearance; the identification from the two is probably easiest by how the leaves are attached on the stem. The Common Sorrel's leaves clasp the stem as shown in the photograph, but the Sheep's Sorrel's leaves are mainly on stalks. Common Sorrel is a common sight in open woods and grassy areas around most of Britain and flowers from May to July growing up to 1 metre.

Cuckoo Pint or Lords and Ladies

This plant has a colourful folklore history with its
association with sex. A visit to Bill Oddie's web site will
reveal a humorous description of such associations.
Here are some of its folklore names. Devils and Angels,
Cows and Bulls, Adam and Eve, Naked Boys, Starch Root,
Wake Robin, and Jack in the Pulpit. Purple spotted leaves
appear in the spring, followed by the purple flower
called the spadex which is enclosed in a hood called
the spathe. It is this appearance that has attracted its
connotations with the lusty side of life. The Victorians
tried to disguise this image of association by calling the
plant Our Lord and Lady by suggesting that the spathe

... Cuckoo Pint or Lords and Ladies

was a cloak to shield Jesus - the spadex. When pollinated by insects the green berries appear then turn red when mature, as shown below, and remain while the leaves wither away. These berries are very poisonous and on no account should they be ingested. They contain oxalates of Saponins which have needle shaped crystals which can cause massive discomfort if eaten. However the root has been roasted and ground and sold under the name of Portland Sago something like a Salop or Salep, a working class drink before we knew of tea and coffee. It has also been used as a substitute for arrowroot, and used as a starch, hence the name Starch Root. Cuckoo Pint will appear from May onwards preferring a shady damp habitat, growing to a height of 40cms.

Dog Rose

A vigorous climber of hedgerows with a magnificent scent. It is a little sad that this sweet smelling rose should be called a Dog Rose, because Dog in the world of flowers means worthless which this plant certainly is not. The ancient Greeks believed that the roots could be a cure after being bitten by a mad dog. The Romans then adopted the name Rosa canina which is then translated directly into English, that is, the Dog Rose. The plant has a valuable medical contribution to generations of children being brought up on Rose Hip Syrup which is rich in vitamin C. The plant will be at its finest during the months of June and July.

Great Willowherb

It is the largest of our Willowherbs but it often gets
overshadowed by The Rose Bay variety, probably because
the Great Willowherb's habitat is that of wet grassland,
ditches, ponds and by the edges of rivers. It spreads by
seed and by its fleshy rhizomes growing under the water
or mud and forming huge dense stands and thickets,
often crowding out other plants. It is a hairy plant. Its
species botanical name is hirsutum which is Latin for
hairy, so is also known as the Great Hairy Willowherb.
Other names are Codlins and Cream, Apple Pie and
Cherry Pie which refer to the pink and cream flowers.
Codlins are cooking apples which were boiled in milk and
eaten with cream. The Great Willowherb reaches a height
of over 2 metres and flowers from July to September.

Hardheads or Knapweed

The shape of the flower heads has given this plant its common name. The flowers are knob shaped and hard and knap means knob. Its botanical name is Centaurea nigra. The species name nigra is Latin for black and this is referring to the black patterning on the calyx which is showing as the dark part of the flower head shown in the photograph below. It is thought that Centaurea is so called because it is named after Chiron the wisest of the Centaurs who used the plant to heal wounds. It is bound up in Greek mythology. It has also had a long association as part of the herbalist's armoury. It has been used to alleviate cuts, bruises, sore throats and scabs, and has even been rubbed on cows udders after a calving. It is a plant that grows in coarse grassland and roadsides, reaching a height of 60cms and can be seen from June to September.

Hedge Woundwort

One of the few plants seemingly with no folklore attachment. It is a tall hairy plant ranging from 70-120cms, and, as the photograph shows, the hairy heart shaped leaves are borne in opposite pairs. The lower lip of the flower has white markings. Another means of identification is its smell. When crushed the smell is unbelievably foul. The word 'wound' in the plant gives a clue that it has been used in medicines. The leaves act as an antiseptic and have been used for staunching blood. Since ancient Greek times the plant has had an important place in the apothecary's shop of the time. Recent scientific analysis does reveal that the plant does have useful volatile oils. Goats and sheep like to eat Woundwort, but not apparently cattle and pigs. It is a common plant of woods, hedges and ditches, flowering from June to August.

Hemp Agrimony

Hemp Agrimony is a member of the Daisy family found in streams, marshes, and wet woodlands growing well in excess of 1200cm. It has reddish stems, bright green leaves growing in opposite pairs and a cluster of tight flat topped red flowers. Its botanical name is Eupatorium cannabinum. Its generic name comes from Eupator Mithridates V1, King of Pontus, an ancient civilisation of Asia, way back a 100 years or more BC. It was Mithridates who discovered the medical properties of Hemp Agrimony and the plant is named after him. Its species name comes from the Latin meaning cannabis as the leaves are similar. The medical qualities of the plant have been described as 'rough', that is, extracts had to be used with caution, as it had violent effects, but it was used as a poultice, and mixed with lard to heal wounds. The plant flowers from July onwards.

Herb Robert

Also known as Red Robin, Death come Quickly, Bloodwort, Wren's Flower, Puck, Robin-in-the-Hedge and Granny thread the Needle. There are others. Folklore myth says that any flowers called Robin have associations with death and fairies. Robin is short for Robert. Its name of Geranium robertianum means crane and red, the crane being the seed pods looking like a cranes bill and red referring to the stalks. Like all in the Geranium family it is also called the Storksbill. It is a strong smelling plant with reddish stems and fern like leaves, the fresh leaves having a smell of burning tyres. Its redness implies that it could be a cure for blood disorders, and it has indeed been used to cure toothache, nosebleeds, ulcers, and mouth bleeding, and when crushed and applied to the body it will act as a mosquito repellent. Herb Robert prefers shady places, in hedges, walls, rocks and similar, has a long season in flower from April to December, reaching a height of 50cms.

Himalayan Balsam

Introduced from its native land, the Himalayas in 1839, it was first grown in greenhouses and then escaped and has now become naturalised all over Britain. It has many names including Policeman's Helmet, Bobby Tops, and Gnome's Hatstand. Its botanical name is Impatiens glandulifera which are both Latin words, the first name for impatient and, in the second word, glandis means gland and fera to bear. This name has come about because its method of seed dispersal is aggressive. When the seeds are ripe and, as there can be up to eight hundred seeds per plant each measuring 30mm x 8mm, when they are disturbed they will explode scattering the seeds up to 7metres. These seeds are usually spread by water and can remain viable up to two years. The flower itself has glands which produce sticky strong nectar which attracts the pollinators, the consequence being that this plant outcompetes many of the others. It is also tolerant to a poor light source so shades out other vegetation so, now, the authorities have recognised the Himalayan Balsam as an invasive species weed. It will be found by streams and rivers flowering from June to October growing well in excess of 2 metres.

Honeysuckle

The Honeysuckle is a familiar sight in hedgerows. Here is a climbing plant which entwines itself clockwise (unlike the bindweeds which entwine anti-clockwise) around adjacent growth, often so tight to deform that ensnared plant. It is also called Woodbine, an apt description. Honeysuckle leaves are one of the first to appear in the hedgerows often as early as December, and when it flowers around June the colour deepens after being pollinated. The rich scent of the flower is more prominent at night when the flower is visited by long tongued moths and this long tongue is essential if the nectar is to be extracted as the petal tube is long. It is also the food source of the caterpillars of the White Admiral butterfly. The plant has been used by herbalists as a cure for headaches, asthma and other respiratory ailments, but its romantic associations are what the plant is remembered by. There is an old folklore tale that if Honeysuckle is brought into a house a wedding will follow. It is a tall plant flowering well into the year. Be aware, because the fruits of the Honeysuckle are poisonous.

Meadow Cranesbill

Its name is Geranium pratense. Geronus is Greek for crane and pratense is the Latin meaning of meadows. It is one of our strikingly blue flowers of meadows, hedgerows and grassy roadsides. It was once known as the Crowfoot Cranesbill, Cranesbill because of the beak over the seeds and Crowfoot because of the leaves resembling those of the Creeping Buttercup. Buttercups used to be called Crowfoots at one time. The wide open blue flowers (another name is Blue Basins) are followed by that charactaristic beaked fruit which split into five segments, each segment containing a seed which act like a spring which coils and disperses the seed. The plant has no recognised economic or medicinal advantages. The only creature that seem to enjoy eating it is the Roe Deer. The Meadow Cranesbill flowers from June and lasts well into the Autumn. The photograph shows the plant growing alongside the large leaves of the Butterbur.

Meadow Saffron

This is both a scarce plant and one of the most poisonous, so either way please treat with respect. It has solitary crocus-like flowers with six orange stamens. Its relation, the August Crocus, has but three. Another name for the plant is Naked Lady. When the plant is in flower the leaves have already died back giving the appearance of having no leaves at all. The photograph below shows the flower in a mass of tangled grass and dying nettles. They are not the leaves of the plant. Meadow Saffron has a long history of its cultivation for uses in medicine as it produces a drug called Colchicine which is well accepted by the medical world with its properties to treat gout and other rheumatic complaints. Its name of Colchicum autumnale indicates that it was recognised to have this drug and of course it grows in the Autumn. It is a plant that is an indicator of ancient woodlands and will be seen in hedgerows in quiet undisturbed places preferring damp moist conditions. It is one of the flowers that bloom in the later months of the year and can be found from September.

Poppy

The Poppy is an agricultural weed hence other names of Corn and Field Poppy. It was once a common sight to see a huge splash of red in the cornfields but due to changing agricultural practices this is becoming rarer. The association of Poppies and corn goes way back to ancient times; Ceres is the Roman Goddess of corn. The Poppy is synonymous with Remembrance Day and it is likely that it is this Poppy that covered the battle fields in France and Belgium after the shelling in the First World War. It is also known as the Flanders Poppy associated with the fallen soldiers. The seeds of the Poppy can lay dormant for decades but when the soil is disturbed, as it was with the shelling on the battlefield and the conditions are right, it will germinate. The Poppy seed

... Poppy

needs light to germinate, which is a sad reflection on the above. The Poppy has four petals and a black centre made up of many black anthers. The petals only last for a day or so and when they fall off the seed capsule forms in the familiar shape of the pepper pot. It has not escaped experimentation in the medical world. It has been used as a herb medicine as a remedy for coughs and colds. The Poppy grows in a variety of habitats from arable fields, dunes and shingle beaches.

Red Campion

Greek mythology has it that Silenus, the merry drunken God of the woods gave his name to this plant, the Silene dioica, The Red Campion. The second part of the scientific name dioica means two houses a reference that the Red Campion is of one sex only, two plants are required to produce seed. Where there are red and white Campions hybridisation often takes place resulting in the pink shades that are seen. Unlike many hybrids these hybrid plants are fertile and again cross pollination takes place with the parent plant, this being called back crossing, hence a huge variation in those shades of pink. Centuries ago it was used to alleviate all sorts of internal ailments. In Wales it was thought to be a plant of the devil, and in the Isle of Man, just don't pick or else! It is a common plant throughout Britain seen in most habitats, reaching a height of around a metre and will be in bloom from May lasting well through the year.

Red Clover

Easily recognised by the big reddish purply flower
head, but more so by the leaves which are trifoliate,
that is, having three leaflets with the leaflets having
that characteristic pale crescent in the outer half of the
leaf. Its botanical name is Trifolium pratense. Trifolium
is Latin for three and pratense meaning 'of meadows'.
The dead flowers turn brown but persist on the plant
protecting the small seed pods from damage. It is a
member of the legume family (the Pea) and is grown as a
fodder crop, valued for its nitrogen fixation capabilities,
commonly known as a green manure crop. Nitrogen
fixation is the ability of the legume family to obtain the
gas nitrogen straight from the air and store it in the
roots by means of nitrogen nodules. This is achieved

by bacteria called 'rhizobium' which infects the plant (harmlessly) and forms an endosymbiotic association with the legume family. It colonises the plant cells with root nodules and here the bacteria converts atmospheric nitrogen to ammonia and produces further compounds beneficial to the plant. This process much reduces the need to use artificial fertilisers. It has had, and still does, have a variety of medicinal purposes including relief from bronchitis, burns and ulcers. Red Clover is the National flower of Denmark and the State flower of Vermont. You will see it from May onward. It is widespread.

Redshank

Mostly described as a sprawling weed, Redshank will
be seen growing within the boundary of Dunstanburgh
Golf Course. Its botanical name is Polygonum maculosa,
Latin words, Poly meaning many and gony for knee. Its
species name used to be called persicaria meaning 'red
dragon' but has been changed. The word maculosa means
spotted, referring to the leaves. It can be identified by
its reddish stems and more certainly by the leaves which
have that brown or black spot which is associated with
a blood stain attributed to Christ's blood from the Cross.
The flowers are a pinkish red and are described as being
held in dense panicles. In medicine, Redshank has been
used as a cure for diarrhoea and other infections and
the young leaves and shoots collected as a vegetable.
Redshank flowers from June onwards, growing in a
variety of habitats, including cultivated soils, waste land,
cracks in pavements and against walls.

Restharrow

The plant's common name means literally 'arrest the harrow'. In the days before tractors it was considered a nuisance because of its woody matted stems and deep roots. It slowed the progress of the horse drawn harrow and other old fashioned farm implements. Another reason it was disliked by farmers was because the leaves when crushed gave off an unpleasant smell and when cattle eat it, it taints the milk so another name for the plant is Camocky. However all is not ill about the plant. Children of yesteryear dug up the roots and ate them like root licorice, hence another name of Wild Licorice. Restharrow grows in rough grassy areas, lime rich soils, shingle beaches and sand dunes. It has a lilac pea like flower (it is a member of the Pea family) and trefoil leaves and will be seen in abundance around Dunstanburgh from June to September..

Rosebay Willowherb

This plant is easily recognisable standing over 1 metre with pinkish purplish flowers. June to September are its best months. It is associated with disturbed ground, the seeds germinating after exposure to high temperatures, hence another name 'Fireweed'. Any rail journey and observation of the embankments will reveal mile upon mile of this plant as it owes its spread to the days of steam. Bombsites during the war were quickly colonised by the Rose Bay, which has earned it yet another name of Bomb Weed. When the plant is seeding it will have recognisable white downy billows of seeds; the capsule splits to release these plumed seeds which disperse freely on the wind. Once established in its new habitat the roots spread out horizontally and will send out new shoots at intervals often crowding out other plants. Its common name Willowherb is because the leaves are shaped like those of the Willow Tree. Its botanical name is Chamaenerion angustifolium. The first name comes from the Greek Chamae meaning on the ground and nerion meaning Rose Bay. The species name comes from the Latin Angusti for narrow and folium for leaved. The plant can be eaten and is known in Canada as Wild Asparagus and is still used in parts of Russia with a concoction of the fungus Fly Agaric to make a potent drink. Fly Agaric is very poisonous!

Scarlet Pimpernel

A plant found on cultivated and waste ground, shingle beaches and dunes. It is a creeping plant with red flowers in pairs growing from a leaf angle. There are times when the colours vary showing pink, blue or violet but the colour red is the most common. It is also known as The Poor Man's Weather Glass, Shepherd's Weather Glass and Change of the Weather, as the flowers only open in the sunshine. When damp and cloudy they close, however when they do flower it is from around 8 am and to bed at 3 pm. Its botanical name is Anagallis arvensis. Anagallis is Greek meaning 'to laugh' as the Greeks thought it cured melancholy and you would laugh after being cured. Its species name is Latin meaning 'of cultivated fields'. The plant has been used medicinally for treatment of various ailments from toothache to snakebites warts and skin eruptions. Baroness Orczy popularised the Scarlet Pimpernel in her novel where the hero Sir Percy Blakeney used the flower as a trademark when he rescued the aristocracy from the guillotine during the French revolution. The plant flowers from April to October and although it tends to creep along the ground can attain a height of 50cms. It is shown here growing in waste ground alongside the Medick.

Tufted Vetch

Also known as Huggaback, Mouse Pease, Flowers and Thumbs, Cow Vetch and Bird Vetch, this is an attractive plant of hedgerows with showy flower heads holding up to forty blueish purple flowers themselves growing in symmetrical rows from long trailing stems. It is a sprawling plant similar to the Pea in growth habits, with branched tendrils that enables it to clamber through the undergrowth reaching heights well over two metres and often crowding out and 'strangling' smaller plants. It is a green manure crop and like other leguminous plants it has nitrogen fixing properties. (See the Red Clover for a basic explanation of this). Birds are fond of the seeds, hence Bird Vetch. They also eat the foliage. It is a common plant of grassland and hedgerows and will flower from June to August.

Water Avens

As the name suggests it is a plant that favours a damp habitat and it will be found in wet meadows, ditches, bogs and similar. It has nodding orange pink flowers which has invited other folklore names. Here are a few of them. Billy's Buttons, Soldiers Buttons, Drooping Avens, Nodding Avens, Water Flower, Indian Chocolate and Cure All. The name Cure All rightly suggests it has been used to alleviate a variety of ailments, although it is generally agreed it has little to offer medicinally as the name might suggest. The roots have the aroma of cloves and have been used to flavour beer. The Water Aven is related to the Wood Aven, a yellow flower and when in proximity has been known to hybridise. Primarily it is pollinated by bees and insects but as the plant matures the stamens elongate to ensure pollination. The seeds are bur-like and are dispersed by wind and by adherence to the fur of small mammals. The plant flowers from May to September growing up to 40cms.

Watermint

Mentha aquatica is its botanical name which descibes it perfectly. Both are Latin names meaning Mint and Water. It is a plant of fens, marshes, ponds and other similar habitats, growing alongside the Mare's Tail and the Spearwort. It is a species that is common throughout Britain. Watermint is the forerunner of today's air freshener, and the uses of this plant go back to the Stone Age. The Romans used to cultivate it for its aromatic value, and the Greeks used it in their bath water. As a strewing herb it was common for it to cover floors of functions, pleasure facilities and bed chambers. There are many hybrids stemming from Watermint, for example Ginger and Apple Mint, and the perfumery and medical industries have produced dozens of commodities which are in everyday use. Mint Tea , Mint Jelly, Chewing Gum, Toothpastes, and Mouthwashes are just but a few. The plant has reddish- green square stems, oval hairy leaves with the flowers arranged immediately above the leaves. Its flowering time is from July to October.

Wild Strawberry

Its common name goes way back to Anglo-Saxon times and there are a number of explanations how it originated: 'straw' meaning to strew over the ground in reference to its creeping runners, or the pips on the fruit, or just small particles of chaff. Its name of Fragaria vesca however is Latin for scent and little. The Wild Strawberry can be found in a number of habitats such as woods, scrub and grassland and even growing in stone walls. It is the refuge and food plant of numerous slugs, snails and insects and will be seen growing alongside Violets, the Ivy and other grasses. Garden strawberries were first grown in France in the 18th century and are a hybrid between the Chilean and American variety. Beware!, the leaves of the cultivated variety are poisonous, however, the Wild Strawberry leaves have been used as a remedy for numerous ailments which include stomach upsets, liver complaints, gall stones and arthritis. The leaves are supposed to help Guinea Pigs that are off colour but please do not try any experiments of this nature at home. The plant flowers from April to July and grows up to 30cms.

Fox and Cubs

It is a native of the mountains of Europe where it grows close to 3000 metres and in some parts of Europe it enjoys the status of being protected. It was introduced into the U.K. because of its attractive orange flowers but has escaped and now grows prolifically in most of the country. It has a vigorous root system which is hard to eradicate. It is also known as the Orange Hawkweed, the Devil's Paintbrush and Grim the Collier. The last name refers to the stiff black hairs on the leaves and stem which give it the appearance of being covered in coal dust. Its common name is likely to be derived from the shape of the flower head with the smaller developing flowers nestling around mother. This plant is a member of the Hawkweed group which include the Cat's Ear and many Hawkbits and Hawkbeards. Fox and Cubs is easy to identify by its colour but the others can become difficult and experts will usually identify them by the leaves. The plant flowers from June growing to a height of 35cms.

Bittersweet or Woody Nightshade

On no Account eat any of this plant. The whole plant is poisonous. The flowers, berries, foliage, the whole lot! Birds eat the berries hence its dispersal. Its botanical name is Solanum dulcamar. Solanum is from the Latin word solamen meaning solace or comfort due to the plants narcotic properties. Dulcamar is from two Latin words meaning sweet and bitter hence accounting for its name. It is a woody plant that does not have tendrils or hooks to climb. It literally climbs through and over obstacles, and on sand dunes it just sprawls. The small purplish flowers have backward facing petals with a central yellow cone (the anther) and can be seen in a number of habitats, from flooded woody areas to sandy shingle beaches. It flowers from May onwards and can attain height well in excess of 2 metres. The flowers can be mistaken for that of the deadly Nightshade (also poisonous) but the Deadly Nightshade has small egg shaped black fruits. The Bittersweets are reddish scarlet and shiny. The plant belongs to a family which includes the Potato and the Tomato which provide valuable medicines and foods so it may be expected, because of the toxins present in this plant, it has been used for medical purposes. The alleviation of rheumatism to name but one.

Creeping Thistle

Its botanical name is Cirsium arvense. Cirsium is Latin for the thistle family and arvense meaning of cultivated ground, and the old English word 'Thistel' means to prick. Here is a thistle that is so successful that it has been listed under the weeds control order of 1959. It is invasive and persistent. The smallest fragment of the root will regenerate within a matter of weeks. The plant not only relies on the seeds to reproduce, but will send a creeping root system which will

send up a new plant some distance away from the parent plant. Most plants of this thistle have male and female flowers; the male flowers are round and the female's flowers oblong. Although classified as an invasive weed the Creeping Thistle is a splendid sight to the eyes with its purple flower heads which also attract a host of butterflies. One of its other names is the Creeping Plume Thistle. The seeds do have useful oils but this attribute has not been exploited. The plant flowers from June onwards reaching a height of 120cm.

Ground Ivy

Also known as Alehoof and Gill-over-the-Ground because, before the introduction of the Hop in the 16th century Ground Ivy was used to flavour ale due to its strong aromatic properties. Gill House is an old term for an Ale House. Other names include Field Balm, Hay Maids, Tunhoof, Run away Robin and Creeping Charlie. It is a member of the Mint family. Its botanical name is

Glechoma hederacea, the former word coming from the Greek glechom meaning mint, and the species name is the Latin for ivy-like. Ground Ivy is one of the first of the spring plants and is considered to be an invasive plant, crowding others out. It spreads by both seeding and by the stems rooting if the nodes touch the ground. The plant has been used to flavour soups and salad, and as a remedy for digestive disorder. A tonic made by boiling the leaves is called Gill Tea. For a cure for catarrh, this is done by putting the plants juices up the nostrils, or by preparing a snuff from the dried leaves. This photograph was taken on the same site as the Moschatel, but about four weeks after the Moschatel's time span. See Ground Ivy as early as March growing in hedgerows and similar.

Purple Loosestrife

Purple Loosestrife is an aggressive plant capable of forming colonies. It was introduced to the U.S.A. early in the 19th century and is recognised as a serious pest costing millions of dollars to keep under control. It degrades wetlands, which harbour a host of wildlife by obliterating the site under a sea of purple flowers. Where fish spawn and rice is sown these areas become ravaged by the plant. Its name is Lythrum salicaria, the former word coming from Greek for blood and  the species name is the Latin Solix meaning willow-like. This is a reference to its long willow type leaves growing in opposite pairs up the reddish square stems. This is a reliable way to identify the plant. There is little evidence that it has proved to be of great benefit in the medical world but it is rich in tannins and has been used as an alternative to Oak bark for tanning leather. The plant will grow in most places but mainly in damp margins and verges, flowering from June to August and growing to a height of 1.5 metres.

Seaside Centaury

This is a rare plant restricted to the coasts of North East England, Wales and Scotland. It is smaller than the Common Centaury growing up to 25cms but unlike the pink flowers of its relative these are a rich deep purple held on an upright stout stem with fleshy leaves. As its name suggests it is a plant of the seaside and likes sand dunes, gravelly and stony sites. The plant flowers from July to August.

Self Heal

Also known as Hook Heal, Carpenter's Herb and Sickly Wort. Its common name has associations with scythes and sickles as the plant had a reputation of having the powers to heal wounds sustained by these tools of the land. The flower shape is also believed to be in the form of a hook, and billhooks were another tool likely to cause injury. Its botanical name  is Prunella vulgaris. Its generic name originates from a German name for a sore throat, and it was used in ancient times as a cure for tonsillitis and sore throats. It is recognised as having properties to lower the blood pressure and as an antibiotic. Its species name, like so many other plants is the Latin for 'common'. It has not escaped the kitchen; it can be eaten as a salad. Self Heal will be found in grassland and open spaces among the shorter grasses where the flowers are usually purple and with the bright shiny leaves being borne in opposite pairs. Self Heal flowers from June onwards reaching a height of 30cms.

Spear Thistle

The Scottish Tourist Board uses this distinctive thistle as their promotional emblem. It is the leaves that give it its name. They do resemble spears and they are very spiny, sharp with yellow tipped spikes. It is a tall imposing plant, seen from May onwards, often reaching heights in excess of 150cm, bearing solitary flowers atop the stems. The stems have spiny wings.

Although an imposing plant its name does not do it justice. Its botanical name is Cirsium vulgare, which is Latin meaning family of thistles and common. It has the infamous honour of being designated an 'injurious weed' under the U.K. Weeds Act of 1959. The Spear Thistle will be found in most habitats, including cultivated pastures, wasteland and even shingle beaches. Unlike its cousin the Common or Creeping Thistle its spread is through seeding and not root fragments. It is a valuable nectar source to many insects, and the mature seeds are a food source for Goldfinches, Greenfinches and Linnets. It has had its medicinal uses. An infusion of the plant (except the roots) is said to be a good general tonic, and the stems can be peeled, steamed and boiled.

Thyme

Ancient Egyptians used Thyme for embalming, the Greeks used it as a form of bath salt, and it is thought that the Romans (amongst others) used it to flavour cheeses and

liqueurs, and as an incense to assure a safe passage to the next life. Its name is Thymus polytrichus, Thymus coming from the Greek Thumon, to fumigate, that is in the sacrificial sense. Polytrichus is Latin for hairy. Of recent times researchers have claimed that an extract from the herb could be a more effective cure for acne than the traditional anti-acne creams. From reports read it appears the debate continues. Other names for the plant include Creeping Thyme, Lemon Thyme and Mother of Thyme, and will be seen as a mat forming plant with creeping rooting runners and sprawling flowering stems, with reddish purple flowers. Along with Mint and Sage it is one of the most well-known culinary herbs - it is a member of the Mint family. Its leaves contain 'thymol', an oil which has preservative and antiseptic qualities, and is an active element in disinfectants and mouthwashes. Thyme flowers from June onwards and will be found on dry grasslands and heaths and dunes.

Bluebell (England)
Wild Hyacinth (Scotland)

A Bluebell wood is a magnificent sight in both sight and smell, and in this locality there is an encouraging display mainly covering the Northern part of the Golf course. The plant is native to North Western Europe and nowhere else in the world can be found a sight of a Bluebell wood. The Bluebell can survive its flowers being picked, but, if the leaves are trampled upon and crushed, the plant may well die as the leaves provide the food for the bulbs in the form of sugar and starch. In Elizabethan days the starch from the bulbs was used to stiffen their elaborate ruffs, cuffs and other exotic clothing worn in those days. It was also used to make glue. It is one of the most easily recognised plants with erect stems and clusters of nodding scented bell shaped flowers. On occasions the blossoms are not always blue. The plant will also bear pink or white flowers. The plant will flower from April to June.

Broad Leaved Willowherb

It is a persistent weed not much cared for when invading gardens. It is efficient at wind seed dispersal, and its creeping stems root separately and remain underground when the plant is pulled out. All Willowherbs get their common name from the slender stems and leaves likened to the Willow Tree, but as the name suggests the Broad Leaf variety has the broadest leaves. The plant likes damp woodland, hedgerows and will often be seen by walls and cracked paving. The stalk and leaves are hairless and the lilac coloured flowers are solitary arising from the junction of the leaf and stem. It is a food source of a number of butterflies- several of the Comets, the Small Phoenix and the Striped Hawk Moth. To us it has little value as a food or as a medicine but it does have astringent properties. The plant flowers from May to August and gains a height to around 40cms.

Bugle

A rich blue plant with each flower spike growing on top
of a pair of dark green leaves. Bugle flowers from May
onwards, growing to a height of 25cms preferring a shady
moist environment. It has many folklore names, Blue
Bugle, Bugleher, Carpet Bungleweed and Burgundy Lace.
It is the plant of the Duke of Burgundy butterfly. It is also
known as the Carpenters Herb as it was supposed to stop
bleeding when the carpenter had a mishap. Apparantly,
an infusion of peppermint and Bugle is still used today
for relief of dyspepsia and gall bladder problems. The
origin of the Bugle's name is somewhat vague, but its
name is probably a corruption of one of the plants earlier
names, bugula, abija, or abuga. Its Latin name Aajuga
seems to uphold this theory. Besides seed dispersal the
plant also spreads by means of the stem touching the
ground when it then takes root and thus can have far
reaching runners.

Butterwort

Also Known as Bog Violet, its habitat is that of damp moors heaths and bogs. It is one of our carnivorous plants supplementing its nutritional needs where its environment is lacking in salts and minerals. It is easily identified by the rosette of yellowish green leaves, which are fleshy, slimy and curled at the edges. Its botanical name is Pinguicula vulgaris where Pingus is Latin for the leaves being greasy and fat, whilst vulgaris is Latin for common. An insect landing on the leaves is held by the stickiness of the leaves. Their struggle triggers the leaf to curl up, the insect is trapped and the process of digestion begins. When over, the process starts again. As the name suggests Butterwort used to be used to curdle milk for butter. You can find the plant from May to July, with its single purple flowers held on long stalks up to 15cm.

Common Comfrey

The medicinal properties of this plant go way back to ancient Greek and Roman times. Other names include Knitbone and Boneset. When the roots are dug up, grated and made into a sludge and applied to the broken limb it sets similar to the plaster of Paris used today. The 'common' in the name comes from the Latin to 'conferre', to bring together. Generally, the Comfrey was considered good for anything that ailed you, and has been much used in proprietary medicines to treat eczema, mastitis, and ulcers, and in more recent times extracts from the roots have been used to treat coughs and sneezes. As with many plants it has been eaten as a vegetable, in this case lightly boiled like spinach. It is a rough hairy plant liking the moist ground of rivers and ditches, reaching a height to 120cm with bell shaped drooping clusters of white blue and pink flowers. It is in bloom from May to July.

Common Milkwort

A plant which is easily overlooked as it is usually dwarfed by grasses and other plants. It is seen here in some scrub rubbing shoulders with young Gorse shrubs, solitary Bluebells, the Dog Violet and Lady's Smock. Its botanical name is Polygala vulgaris. Polygala is made up of two Greek words, Poly meaning many and Gala meaning milk. Vulgaris, as with many plants is the Latin meaning common. It is a small plant growing up to 30cms and will be seen in colours ranging from white, pink, blue and purple. This may account for another name of 'four sisters'. It is also known as the Rogation plant, where the Milkwort was the flower in garlands worn by the participants in crop blessing rituals. Milkwort as the name suggests had to have some folklore history in

relation to milk. Infusions of the plant were supposed
to increase nursing mother's milk, although apparently
this has not been substantiated. If wondering why such a
plant should be considered to possess such qualities, it is
the flowers which resemble udders. Closer examination
of the flower will show that the colour comes from
large sepals and not so much from the petals which are
partly hidden and fused into a tube, with the lower petal
being fringed. It has a close relative, the Heath Milkwort
and the two plants can be identified by the leaves. The
Common Milkwort's leaves grow alternately up the stem
whilst the Heath Milkwort's leaves grow in opposite
pairs. The Milkwort will be seen flowering from May
onwards.

Common Spotted Orchid

This is the most common of our Orchids, and one that can be seen in considerable quantity. The colours of the flowers vary, but in the main are pinkish purple, but they can be recognised by their purple dots and dashes, and of course those spotted leaves. It is a variable species and often crosses with other related plants, and as aforementioned there is a variance of colour even producing white flowering plants which some botanists claim to be another sub-species. The consensus is that they are over classified. If it is a warm spring the Orchids will appear in May otherwise June or even July, and can be found mostly anywhere, in hedgerows, grassland, heaths and damp habitats such as ponds and streams.

Common Storksbill

Erodium circutarium is its name. The first word is Greek for Heron, and the latter is the Latin for round referring to the fruit. It is a plant that likes sandy grasslands and is common around the coast of Britain. It is easily spotted and readily identified by its fern- like leaves. You can find it in the dune slacks around Dunstaburgh from May onwards growing to a height of 40cms. It has an unusual method of seeding. The long beaked fruit (where it gets its common name) splits and twists from the base, each segment carrying a seed. This 'corkscrew' end behaves as a corkscrew determined by the humidity at the time, expanding and contracting so screwing the seed into the ground until the correct depth for shooting is obtained. Backward facing hairs prevent the seed from remerging. The short life of the flowers is also unusual; from opening in the morning they may be pollinated and have dropped their petals by noon. Storksbill has been used to stem bleeding and the whole plant can be eaten, mainly the young leaves used in salads.

Common Vetch

This Vetch can be distinguished from the other Vetches as it usually has a solitary or a pair of stalkless flowers with a black spot at the base. This plant twines its way through grass and other plants enabling it to gain a height up to 1metre. The other related species to this plant are the Bush and Tufted Vetch. The Common Vetch shown here has its solitary flower; the Bush Vetch has clusters of two  to six flowers and the Tufted Vetch clusters of ten to forty flowers. The Vetch here is fairly widespread and generally found in grassy shrubby places, hedgerows or similar. As with others of the Legume family it is a nitrogen fixation plant and is a valued farming commodity. Its botanical name is Vicia sativa. Vicia is Latin for its plant name of Vetch and sativa, its species name is Latin for cultivated. On the continent this plant is cultivated for animal fodder and green manure. It has been part of the human diet (and still is). Carbonised remains have been found at early Neolithic sites in countries such as Turkey, Syria and Bulgaria. The Vetches will be seen in flower from May onwards.

Dog Violet

Once known as the Viola canina (canine as in dog) but is now known as the Viola riviniana. The Viola canina is the Heath Dog Violet. Here is a plant that flowers as early as March and it is common in pastures, woods, hedges, heaths, grasslands and rocky areas. The term 'dog' when applied to plants is a way of describing the plant as being in some form inferior to its relatives. In this case the plant has no scent compared to the Sweet Violet. Other examples of this derogatory term are the Dog Rose, which is not a cultivated rose, or the Dogwood that bears fruit that should not be eaten. However this cheerful Violet heralds the oncoming of spring. Flowering in the early months of the year means that insect pollinators are relatively scarce so this particular species grows self-pollinating flowers that remain unopened until the summer. It is seen all over the Dunstanburgh area from March onwards.

Dove's Foot Cranesbill

A low growing spreading plant that likes dry soils and will readily be seen in the sand dunes. In the autumn the leaves can turn into varying shades of red due to the production of pigments called Anthocyanins which give trees their Autumnal beauty show. Its common name of Dove's Foot comes from the idea that the leaves look like a Dove's foot, but its botanical of Geranium molle does not relate to the foot at all. Geranium comes from the Greek geranos meaning crane (the bird's bill) and molle is Latin for soft, as the plant has a soft hairy nature. Other names are Soft Cranesbill, Soft Geranium, Cranesbill Geranium and Awnless geranium. The lilac coloured flowers are what is known as being obdurate, that is as the photograph shows there appears to be ten petals but there only five because they are deeply notched. Medicinally, it has had its uses to treat colic, gout, muscle pains, as well as the treatment of open cuts and bruises. The plant grows to 20cms and is long lasting from April to September.

Early Marsh Orchid

This is the most common of the Marsh orchids and is in
abundance around the wetter localities of Dunstanbugh.
Its botanical name is Dactylhoriza incarnata where
dactylos is Greek for finger and is rhiza Greek for root.
Incarnata is Latin meaning pink coloured which is
somewhat confusing when most of the Marsh orchids
here are a rich blue-purple. However, there are, as with
many of the orchids several sub-species with flowers
ranging from pure white to salmon pink and from lilac
to red. This Orchid has unspotted yellowish-green leaves
hooded at the tip, a stout hollow stem holding flowers
that have a red double loop with dots and lines inside. It
likes wet meadows, a non acidic soil, a lover of the sandy
soil of the Machair. Machair is a Gaelic word, and is a

make up, a mixture of different habitats such as beaches, dunes, dune slacks, pastures and marshes. The plant was was once used to make the drink salop. This was a milky beverage that originated in Turkey, its ingrediant the flour from the ground roots of the Orchid species. These starchy tubers made a drink the consistancy of hot chocolate or smooth tapioca, and it is still consumed in Turkey but has somewhat declined due to the plant becoming scarcer. Here in Britain, at the height of its popularty around the early 1700's it was sold as an alternatve to coffee and chocolate – there used to be salop vendors who used to sell it from booths. The Marsh Orchid gows to a height of 20cms and will be seen flowing from May.

Forget-Me-Not

The Forget-me-Not is identified by its pale blue flowers with its yellow central eye. Here is a common flower found all over Britain in woods, cultivated land and dunes. There are other varieties such as the Tufted and Wood, and even a white variety, but shown here is the common blue flowered Forget-me-Not. The shape and hairiness of the plant's leaves are  reflected in its Greek plant name of Myosotis, meaning mouse ear. Another characteristic of this plant is the curvature of the main stem likened to a Scorpion's tail; hence in some regions it is called Scorpion Grass. It is a plant entrenched in folklore legend, the most famous being that of a drowning knight who threw his flowers to his beloved crying "forget me not". This is developed by Shakespeare in Hamlet where Ophelia is drowning in a lake of flowers and she cries 'forget me not,' and this flower, amongst others, is illustrated in the above scene in a painting by Sir John Everett Millais. This painting is now held in the Tate.

THE WILD FLOWERS OF DUNSTANBURGH

Foxglove

A tall unmistakable plant that flowers from June onwards. It is uncertain where the name of Foxglove comes from as it has nothing to do with foxes or gloves. The theory is that it is a corruption of old Anglo Saxon words over the years. In the Southern Counties it is known as Fairy Bells. Its botanical name is Digitalus purpurea, Digitus is the Latin for finger and purpurea means purple. The plant yields a drug called digitalus which is used today in the treatment of heart complaints. It was a physician called William Withering in 1785 who initiated the first scientific examination of plants for herbal medicine, which in 1785 seems a hazardous task to undertake. Needless to say the whole plant is poisonous. The Foxglove stands 1.8 metres with clusters of pink purplish flowers, having maybe up to 70 flowers adorning one side of the stem only. Note the extended lower lobe on the flower tube, this is the landing area for insects and the spots inside the flower are the nectar guides for the insects.

Fumitory

Its botanical name is Fumaria officinalis, where Fumus is Latin for smoke. This is a way of describing the leaves, which are whitish, blue-green and seem to resemble dispersing smoke, and to the acrid smell of gas given off from the roots when pulled up. In America it is known as Fume Root. Its species name officinalis is Latin for medicinal, and it is still used by herbalists in some potions. It has been used as a laxative, detoxifier, and as a lotion treatment for skin conditions. It is still used in some proprietary medicines. The plant likes disturbed waste ground and will be seen flowering showing its purple-lilac coloured flowers (also known as Wax Dolls in the Northern Counties) from May to September reaching a height of 50cm.

Germander Speedwell

According to one's view, the Speedwell is so called because it was widely used medicinally to cure a variety of ailments. In reality it has little medicinal value. When picked or shaken the petals are very easily dislodged from the stem, hence Speedwell, meaning Farewell or Goodbye. Germander is Greek, meaning on the ground, and as for

its botanical name of Veronica chamaedrys, the plants name is named after St.Veronica. The species name comes from the Latin Creeping Speedwell attributed to its ability to facilitate a fast cure. Germander Speedwell is the most common of the Speedwells; all having similar flowers, that is, sky blue, four petalled with the lower petal narrower and smaller. The centre of the flower has a white eye and two stamens extending from within the centre. Again this appearance has brought it many folklore names, Blue Bird's Eye, Bird's Eye Speedwell, or Bonny Bird's Eye. It is a hairy plant with, unusual amongst the Speedwells, two lines of long hairs on opposite sides of the stem. It is a common plant of hedges and grassy places and will be seen from June onwards.

Green Alkanet

A member of the Borage family. It is a bristly hairy plant with the magnificent botanical name of Pentaglottis sempervirens. Penta is Greek for five and glottis means windpipe. The literal translation is 'five tongues always alive'. Its species name comes from the Latin meaning evergreen, a reference to the leaves which will persist well into the frosts of winter. The five tongues refers to the shape of the five blue petals and if you look at the underside of the petals you will see that familiar groove as a tongue has. It is uncertain why this plant was introduced from Europe as it had no recognised medicinal properties although in France it was used to cure nervous disorders. However, its common name Alkanet comes from the Arabic al-henna, meaning a shrub or plant yielding a red dye and, indeed, Egyptian women used to dye their hair and paint their fingernails with this dye. It is considered a garden escape and will be found in damp hedgerows woods and ditches, often quite close to human habitation. It is often found by old monasteries where its rich red pigment was favoured by those members of the cloth for dying their monastic robes. If grown in the garden it is an invasive plant with a vigorous root system and will run amok if not checked. The plant reaches 60cms in height and flowers from May to July.

Harebell

The Harebell is called
the Bluebell in Scotland
and our own Bluebell is
known in Scotland as the
Wild Hyacinth. It is the
family emblem of the Clan
McDonald. Its botanical
name is Campanula
rotundifolia, which are
both Latin names. The
first name means bell and
the second 'round leaved'.
This causes confusion
because when the flower

is in bloom only the lance-shaped leaves are to be seen.
The rosette of basal leaves which are rounded have
withered away. It has a folklore history. Other names for
the Harebell are, Old Man's Bell, (the Old Man being the
devil himself), Devil's Bell, Witch's Thimble and Witch
Bell. In myth the Hare is a witch. In Eire, you pick it
at your peril as it is a fairy plant called the Goblins (or
Puck's thimble). The papery thin thimble like flowers
belies a toughness and resilience in harsh conditions.
When the wind blows it withstands the gusts just as well
as the golfers, and in some cases, better. It flowers later
in the year and will be seen all around Dunstanburgh.
It tolerates dry poor grassland, and can colonise cliffs,
dunes and cracks in walls. Like all campanulas it exudes
white latex when broken. It flowers from June and lasts
well into September growing to a height of 35cms.

Ivy Leaved Toadflax

A plant which traces its origins to the Mediterranean.
Introduced to London in 1640 it was a favourite of
rockery designers but, as with many others, is now
recognised as a garden escape and is found everywhere.
It is a lover of dry stone walls and crevices. It is a
delightful plant with lilac snapdragon-like flowers. The
common name comes from the shape of the leaves being
similar to the Ivy and the botanical name of Cymbalaria
Muralis comes from the Greek and Latin. The former
name is derived from 'Kymbalon' or cymbal referring to
the dimpled leaf, and muralis means 'of walls'. When the
flowers have been fertilised the stalks curve around and
the seed pods are then pushed into cracks and crevices so
ensuring continuing plant spread. The seeds themselves
are ridged so are wedged into cracks until the root can
gain a secure anchor. Medicinally the plant does have
anti-scorbutic properties and the plant yields a yellow
dye. You can see the plant from May onwards lasting well
into late autumn.

Monkshood

A very poisonous plant. Be advised, do not touch it as the toxic alkaloids can be absorbed through the skin. It is also known as Aconite (the poison is Acontine and is classed as an alkaloid toxin), Wolf's Bane, Leopard's Bane, Women's Bane, Devil's Helmet, Blue Rocket, and Helmet Flower. As has been said, it is one of the most toxic plants known to man. Centuries ago the poison was collected and used to kill Wolves and Dogs, hence Wolf's Bane. Where Women's Bane fits in to this picture remains unclear. It is a garden escape and will be found in damp ditches and woodlands. It has conspicuous helmet shaped flowers. It grows up to a height of 2mtrs and will be seen from May onwards.

Pyramidal Orchid

This Orchid is often found growing alongside the Horseshoe Vetch and this is exactly where this one was found, one of many. It is upright and hairless with long lance- shaped leaves, the upper ones becoming smaller. It can be mistaken for the Fragrant Orchid whose flowers are more pinkish but the Pyramidal Orchid does have that distinctive pyramid cluster of flowers. From the seed, tubers develop after four years, another five years for the leaves to develop and several more years after that for the flowers to appear. Like all Orchids its reproduction has a high success rate. Experts suggest up to 95% successful. This is due to the modified stamens which the insects push directly into the stigma of the next flower. Charles Darwin recognised this and described this in his book, 'The Fertilisation of Orchids'. You will see the plant in flower from July, growing to 40cms.

Sea Aster

A plant that is confined to salt marshes, muddy creeks, estuaries and sometimes seen on cliff tops. It is one of the most flavoursome of the foragable plants. The leaves can be boiled and eaten as spinach and you can find it on the shelves in some of the supermarkets. Its name is Aster tripolium both Latin words meaning star  and three veined which refers to the leaves. In the South West it has the name of Summer's Farewell as it produces nectar well into late summer which is a valuable food source for the late butterflies such as the Painted Lady and the Red Admiral. The flowers of the Sea Aster are pale lilac and the leaves are lance- shaped and fleshy with a distinguishable mid rib. The leaves secrete water to combat the battering of salt water the plant receives from the sea. The Michaelmas Daisy is a similar plant. It is a late flowering flower but it is taller and does not have those fleshy leaves. The Michaelmas Daisy was introduced as a garden plant from North America in the 17th century, and is now another garden escape. The Sea Aster has been around a lot longer than the Michaelmas variety. This particular specimen was taken by the causeway, the approach to Holy Island.

Field Scabious

A plant of open grassy hedge banks, dry fields and roadsides which is found throughout Britain. Other common names are Lady's Pin Cushion's, Pins and Needles and Bachelor's Buttons. This latter name is shared by many plants, notably the Marsh Marigold. The name Pin Cushion comes from the resemblance of the male stamens standing up, as can be seen in the photograph. As might be guessed the common name of Scabious comes from the use the plant has had in curing scabies and other diseases of the skin. It was both drunk as an infusion and applied externally as an ointment. Its botanical name of Knautia arvensis does not give any clue to the medicinal properties of the plant. Knautia was a botanist in the 17th century and the species name comes from the Latin for field. Reaching a height of 40cms the Field Scabious flowers from July to September.

Southern Marsh Orchid

Marsh orchids are notoriously difficult to distinguish with any conviction as there are many varieties. They freely hybridise with the Common Spotted and the Heath Orchids. The words often and usually creep into descriptive narrative so adding to the confusion. It is best left to the experts. Here is an example of how doubt can occur. Some authoritative books

say that the Southern Marsh orchid as shown here at Dunstanburgh grows as far North as South West Sweden whilst others say that the Northernmost limit is about as far North as Hadrian's Wall. Where the Southern Orchid reaches its maximum latitude the Northern variety takes its place. However this handsome plant shown here is the Southern variety. These Orchids will attain heights up to 70cms (the Northern Marsh Orchid rarely exceeds 30cms in height) towering over the Marsh and Common Spotted varieties. Here they are shown growing alongside Ribworts, Buttercups, Silverweed, Mare's Tail and grasses. It is growing in a considerably damp area of Dunstanburgh. It is a late flowering plant and will be seen from July to September.

Teasel

The common name comes from people who weave wool and use the dried Teasel flower heads to raise, or tease the nap on the cloth. It is a cultivated plant in Taunton, and is known as the Fullers Teasel. The difference is the spines on the end of the bracts which curve backwards to form hooks. Well in excess of two metres, this tall imposing plant has thorny stems and a cone shaped flower head. The flowers are small and surround the 'cone' giving the appearance of purple rings. Teasel is probably more easily recognised and is more familiar when the plant dies back and we are left with that spectacular skeleton which is often seen in floral displays. Other names include Brushes and Comb, Johnny prick the finger, and has the dubious honour of being

... Teasel

called the Monster Plant. This name comes from the drowning of insects in the rainwater which is collected in the cups which form around the stem by the leaf bases. The insect bodies are broken down and the nutrients absorbed, so making this a partial carnivorous plant. Experiments have shown that adding insects to this 'cup' does increase the seed set but not the plants' size. The scientific name of Dipsacus is from the Greek 'to thirst' which refers to this function. Medical uses are few and have not been proven by any laboratory trials but it has been used to cure warts, an antibiotic, and as eyewash from that water collected at the leaf bases. It is a food source for the Goldfinch, you may well espy. The plant flowers from July to September.

Thrift or Sea Pink

Also known as Marsh Daisy it is a common flower
forming pink cushions around the salt marshes of Britain.
This is the flower that is to be found on the reverse side
of the old three penny bit, the coin minted from 1937
to 1953, but it has nothing to do with being thrifty.
The plant thrives throughout the year and is adapted
to survive in dry, rugged, sandy and saline conditions.
Long roots which can reach down for a constant water
supply enables it to do this. Unlike most plants it has no
recognised medical properties. In fact, it is poisonous if
ingested, but it is a plant that has been cultivated as a
garden flower for centuries. The garden plant has been
hybridised giving shows of brighter pink and even white
flowers. Its species name of maritima means near the sea,
which is well chosen since it is prolific around this area.
Thrift will start flowering from May onwards.

Vipers Buglos

Found on dry soils in grassy areas this is a tall and roughly bristly plant. It has blue flowers, which are pink when in bud, speckled hairy stems, and the flower elongates as the seeds develop. The filaments of the stamens remain red, as the photograph

shows. The striking blue colour has given rise to other names such as Bluebottle, Blue Cat's Tail, and in some parts of the country it has the name of Blue Devil because of its long tap roots to reach for water. This characteristic makes it hard to eradicate. The name Vipers immediately suggests that it has something to do with snakes, and it was indeed supposed to cure snakebites. A somewhat imaginable resemblance of the flower head to a snake's head gives some sort of credibility to this idea. The Bugloss in the name comes from the Greek for Ox Tongue, associated with the rough tongue shaped leaves. Herbalists found that an infusion promoted nursing mothers milk, as well as a remedy for lumbago and for driving away the depression of melancholy or sadness. Growing up to 1 metre in height it will be seen in flower from May to August. This particular specimen was taken on Holy Island where they are prolific.

Wild Pansy

This is the plant from which the garden pansies are derived. Horticulturists have hybridised the species to produce the large variety which we are familiar with. The Wild Pansy has a much smaller flower, around 10mm across and grows to a height of 30cms. It is common

throughout Britain on cultivated, waste land, dunes and scrub. The plants name is Viola tricolor. The species name meaning 'three coloured', which refers to the three colours of the flower, which may be a combination of yellow and blue or even pink. It is usually a combination or either two or three colours. The Pansy is also associated with love having folk lore names such as Love in Idleness, Heart's Ease, Heart's Delight, Tickle my Fancy, Three Faces in a Hood, and Kiss me Quick. There are many others. Pansies get their name from the French for thoughts, 'penseees', from their habit of leaning forward as if deep in thought. As the name of Heart's Ease suggests it has a long history in the apothecaries shop as a cure of many complaints such as asthma, epilepsy, eczema, bronchitis and colds. The flowers have also been used to make dyes. See the Pansy from April onwards and around Dunstanburgh; it likes the edges of corn fields.

Butterbur

An instantly recognisable plant of wet places, ditches, riverbanks and marshes. You can see it from March onwards. The large rhubarb type leaf (it is also known as Wild Rhubarb) reaches up to 1 metre across and as the name suggests tradition has it that they have been used to wrap butter. The plant's name Petasites comes from the Greek petusos meaning a broad rimmed hat, so it can be assumed that the leaves have also been used as hats. Its species name

of hybridis is Latin for hybrid which is fitting as there are few plants that look like this. Butterbur is related to the Coltsfoot and is often called Sweet Coltsfoot and like the Coltsfoot the flower emerges before the leaves. The flower heads normally seen are male. The female plant has more flower heads which elongate to 60 cm, but the female plants are restricted in their location. The plant spreads by creeping rhizome roots. The roots have been ground to powder and used to remove spots and blemishes but, unusually for most plants, it would appear that the Butterbur has not been used as a food source.

Crosswort

See this plant and it will indicate a lime rich soil. Plants such as this are known as Calcicoles, that is, they are unable to tolerate lime poor soils. The opposite side of the coin are the Calcifuges. These plants cannot tolerate lime and the Heathers are an example. This is a softly haired plant with small yellow flowers, and as the name suggests the word cross refers to

the leaves which are at right angles up the stem; the stem itself is four angled. Its botanical name of Galium cruciata come from the Greek Gala meaning milk, and cruciata meaning cross shaped leaves. It has been used as a rennet hence milk. The suffix 'wort' in plants usually means that they have been used for medical or culinary use and indeed a variant of Crosswort has been used as rennet. Because the leaves are in the form of a cross it was once regarded as a healer of wounds. Crosswort flowers from May to June; it reaches a height of 60cms, and will be found on well drained grassy banks.

Curled Dock

A common plant found in any number of habitats, waste and cultivated ground, heaths and pebbly beaches. More often than not growing next to it will be some Stinging Nettles where nature has provided its own antidote to the sting, the Dock Leaf. As can be seen by the harsh environment depicted in the photograph it is a tough long rooted persistent perennial and has been determined as an injurious weed. The lance shaped leaves have pronounced wavy edges hence its common name Curled Dock. Its botanical name of Rumex crispus are both Latin words meaning Sorrel and wrinkly, and as in the other Sorrels the leaves have been eaten and used for flavourings in soups and fish dishes. Like the Butterbur it was one of the large leaved plants used to wrap foodstuffs in, butter being one of them so it is sometimes known as Butter Dock. The plant grows up to 1mtr and when fruiting will take on that familiar reddish hue.

Dog's Mercury

This is an extremely
poisonous plant
to both humans
and animals. It was
once called Bad
Henry, as opposed
to Good King Henry,
a similar looking
plant but one that
could be eaten. It
is found mainly
in woodlands but
will be seen in
hedgerows. It is said

that the plant is named after Mercury. Its botanical name
is Mercurialis perennis Mercury being the messenger of
the Gods, so it might have been expected to have some
use but it has had very little. Medicinally it has been used
for the alleviation of diarrhoea, dropsy, rheumatism,
and internal complaints, however, the leaves must never
be eaten. The word 'Dog' in plants means inferior in
some respect and in this case it might be correct. The
plant has a fetid smell likened to that of rotting fish. The
purpose of this smell to attract midges which are mainly
responsible for the plant's pollination. The male and
female flowers are on separate plants. The male flowers
are on upright tassel like spikes, and the female flowers
are in small clusters on long stalks. It is a member of the
spurge family, and will be seen flowering from February
to May growing to a height of 50cms.

Lady's Mantle

Alchemilla vulgaris is its botanical name, its generic name derived from the Arabic word alkemelych meaning alchemist. It has had a long association with the alchemists, the plant having strong astringent qualities. Vulgaris is the Latin word for common. The common name is in reference to the Virgin Mary, to whom the plant is dedicated, but this plant has also had uses in curing women's complaints and one tradition was to restore the sagging bosoms of these ladies to their former glory. The leaves are shaped like ladies' capes which gather drops or small pools of dew. Because of this, when other plants had none, the plant was thought to have magic properties and all sorts of experiments were conducted to bring about that elusive pot of gold. When a plant can't lose vapour through natural loss, water is forced out of holes in the leaf. This process is called guttation. The plant grows extensively, found in hedgerows, ditches, and even against walls. See the plant flowering from May onwards.

Lesser Burdock

Generations of children have thrown these burs at one another. After the flower dries out the hooked bracts transport the entire seed to promote its spread. Like the plant Cleavers it has Velcro qualities. Because of this feature it has attracted many names such as Sticky Buttons, Burweed, Louse Bur, Cuckoo Button and Wild Rhubarb. This last name refers to the large leaves. Its botanical name is Arctium minus, the first name is Greek meaning bear, since the plant is hairy like a bear, and the species name minus comes from the Latin for lesser. It is a tall plant often reaching a height of 2 metres, with large leaves which are hairy on the underside. It flowers from June to September. It has a preference for being close to human activity and will often be found in farmyards, waste ground and growing alongside walls. It has been used as a food plant; the stalks can be peeled and cooked similar to cooking spinach. The oil extracted from the plant is supposed to promote hair growth.

Mare's Tail

An oxygenating aquatic plant found in ponds, shallow rivers and marshes. It can also absorb methane so improving the quality of the air around its growing habitat. Its rhizome spreading roots are underwater with the leaves above reaching heights up to 400cm, looking like miniature fir trees or a Monkey Puzzle Tree. The flowers are inconspicuous but produce a cone like structure containing masses of spores. The plant belongs to a family of its own. The Mare's Tails are similar to the Horsetails but the latter are related to the flowerless ferns. It has had its uses in herbal medicine mainly to do with healing wounds, both for internal and external bleeding, ulcers, and as a soothing balm for skin complaints. The plant will be seen from April onwards and it is seen here growing alongside the Marsh Marigold.

Marsh Helleborine

A native wild orchid. Its species name is palustris which is Latin for marsh and that is where it is found, in marshy fields and dune slacks. Dune slacks may seem odd as they relate to sand, but it is in the areas between the dunes where the orchids flourish. In winter these areas become very wet, only drying out in the summer. Marsh Helleborine grows to 50 cms and flowers between July and August. Identification can be made by the leaves which are broad and oval at the base of the stem and narrower higher up. It reproduces by both seed dispersal and by its creeping rhizome. An extensive area can be covered by a rhizome spreading plant. Many of the flowers may well be from one rootstock of that single flower.

Moschatel

An unusual plant being the sole member of its species. It is a small yellowish-green plant only attaining a height of 10cms. It flowers early in the year before it is crowded out by other taller plants such as the Nettles, Crosswort and Ground Ivy. It grows in woods and hedgebanks and when the Month of May is over so will be the Moschatel for another year. This plant is worth looking for as it has an unusual flower structure. The flower head consists of five flowers. One flower faces upwards with four petals and four flowers facing outwards with five petals. This appearance has given rise to other names as Town Hall Clock and The Five Faced Bishop. The latter name, in days of old, was given to a man of the cloth who constantly changed his mind. Its botanical name is Adoxa moschatellina. Adoxa taken from the Greek meaning 'without glory', emphasising that it is a solitary species. The species name is from the Latin Moschata meaning musky smell and its common name also reflects this name. Unsurprisingly the plant is also called Musk Weed. The plant's scent is indeed musky, stronger at dusk or in damp weather, when insects are attracted to its aroma and duly pollinate the plant. However, few seeds are produced, it owes its spread by sending shoots out from its vigorous rootstock.

Mugwort

A plant that is a member of the Daisy and Dandelion family though to look at it is certainly far from obvious. It is an untidy plant that can grow up to 1.3 metres, and is not much to look at but is said to have majical properties. Digging it up would give protection from the plague, lightening, fatigue, sunstroke and protection from wild beasts but only on one day of the year and that is St.John's Eve. In Germany and Holland it is known as the St.John's plant. It has been used as a substitute for hops to flavour beer, and not much more that a hundred years ago infusions of its dried leaves were used as a substitute for tea. It is still used in mainland Europe as a herb for stuffing poultry. Its name Mugwort may not have come from the drinking vessel but from Moughte meaning a moth. It is slightly aromatic when burned and has been used to fumigate sick bays and as a moth repellent. Its species name in vulgaris which is Latin for common and indeed it is common to waste places, usually near to roads and buildings. It is readily recognised by its angular purplish stems, and by the leaves which are glossy green on the upper side, but the underside is covered by a dense cottony down. It will be seen all over Britain flowering from July.

Pineapple Weed

Less known as the Rayless Mayweed this plant is supposed to have been introduced from North America in the late 18th century. Its prolific colonisation of waste places and trampled ground is attributed to its tolerance of  trampling and the adherence of its seeds to car tyres. It is without doubt a pernicious weed. The name more than likely comes from the shape of the flower heads which resemble a pineapple and when crushed decidedly smells of pineapples. Try this, it's true. Its generic name Chamemilla comes from the Greek words meaning 'apples on the ground'. Analysis of the oils extracted from this plant show that the major constituent to be Myrcene, a chemical prized in the perfumery industry. Besides its uses as a perfume the flowers have been used in salads and a bunch of flower heads steeped in hot water and strained, does apparently make a refreshing drink. Its uses in medicine have not been overlooked. It has been used for the relief of stomach upsets, infected sores and fevers. You can see it flowering in all habitats from May to August. It grows to a height of 20cm.

Reedmace

The Reedmace is often mistakenly called the Bulrush. The Bulrush is a sedge and an entirely different species of plant. There are many theories of how this confusion came about, the most likely being an artist's error in naming a painting 'Moses in the Bulrushes' when in fact the Bulrushes were Reedmaces. There  are two species of Reedmace; the Greater and the Lesser. Shown here is the greater with the female flower head about 100mm in length with the male flower head borne directly above the female. In the lesser variety there is a gap of approximately 100mm between them. The plant is a sight of wetlands and marshes and spreads by its invasive rhizomatous root system. Gardeners are warned to restrict their growth to plant pots or it will become a spreading nuisance. The roots are edible and there is evidence from preserved starch grains from ancient stone grinding wheels which indicate that these roots were being eaten in Europe some 30,000 years ago. Reedmace has also been used to stuff mattresses. Baskets and chairs were made out of the leaves and because of the waterproof characteristic of the leaves these have been used to make reed boats. See the plant from June attaining heights well in excess of 2 metres.

Ribwort

Evidence obtained from the pollen preserved in lake sediments and peat bogs has shown that this plant has been around for at least 5000 years, and is still one of the commonest wild flowers of Britain and Europe. The growth of the Ribwort sprouts from the bottom of the plant so is evasive to animals and lawn mowers. Even if the top of the plant is lopped off it will still survive. Ribwort refers to the leaves which are either three or five paralleled veined. Children used and still probably do use the plant's stalk and flower to play a form of conkers, so there are folk lore names as Fighting Cocks or Kemps, Kemps coming from an old English word meaning warrior. Few plants miss being experimented with for a source of food or medicine. A tea made from the leaves works as quite an effective cough medicine. Its botanical name is Plantago lanceolata. Plantago coming from the Latin 'planted' relating to soles of the feet; where the colonists went their feet carried the Ribwort plantain. Ribwort will be seen from May onwards growing in tracks, wasteland and hedges growing to a height of 50cm. Its relative the Hoary Plantain is similar but has much broader leaves.

Stinging Nettle

Everyone knows the Stinging Nettle. From prehistoric days generation after generation has used, hated and needed the nettle. It has been used for clothing, food and medicine, and is still used today for the latter two commodities and no doubt there will be some people, somewhere in the world making use of the nettle fibres to make some sort of cloth. Its scientific name is Urtica dioica, both Latin words. Uro is to burn and dioica meaning of two houses. In other words there are male and female plants the same as the red Campion where its species name is also dioica. Below shows a photograph of the male plant whose flowers droop catkin-like, whilst the female flowers hang in clusters. When the male flowers are mature they burst to release the pollen.

... Stinging Nettle

The stinging comes from small hairs on the plant. They are very fine, like hypodermic needles, and can pierce the skin and then break off. The hollow stinging hairs are called Trichomes, and when the skin is pierced histamines and other chemicals are released resulting in a burning sensation that can last for hours or even days. All parts of the nettle are used and are widely available in a range of ointments, tinctures and herbal extracts. Because of its many nutrients it is traditionally used as a spring tonic and still today the young leaves are boiled and eaten. Steaming kills the 'sting' and we have all heard of nettle wine. The plant grows everywhere and is seen most of the year and given good conditions there can be huge colonies of them reaching heights well in excess of 150cms.

Sun Spurge

One of its other names
is 'Madwoman's Milk',
so called because the
plant's sap is like a latex
and is very poisonous.
If ingested it can cause
extreme pain in the
mouth due to the volatile
oils and alkaloids- it a
flower cocktail of harmful
substances and even
when the plant is dried

these toxins remain. The ingredients are still extracted
today and used in the pharmaceutical industry, and is
still used in traditional Chinese medicine. In the middle
of the 20th century it was widely uses to stem the growth
of warts. It stifled the wart not allowing it to breathe. Its
botanical name is Euphorbia helioscopia, the plant being
named after Euphorbus, a physician in the 1st century.
The species name comes from two Greek words meaning
to 'look at the sun', which is probably due to the flowers
which are looking upwards at the sun. The seeds are
dispersed by the capsule splitting with a sharp crack and
firing the ripe fruits asunder. However the seed may not
germinate where first landed. The seeds have oil which
ants find irresistible and these creatures carry the seed
off, eat the oil, and leave the seed further afield. It is an
early flowering plant, seen here with young Nettles and
when the Nettles have matured the Sun Spurge will have
been crowded out to wait for the following year.

Twayblade

So named because of its
two distinctive and large
basal leaves situated in
opposite pairs suspended
above the ground. Tway
is old English for two,
hence Twayblade. It used
to be called Martigon,
Turkish for hat. The
plant is common around
Britain both in woods,
meadows, scrubland and
sand dunes and will be
seen close to the dunes of
Dunstanburgh. It is often

overlooked because of its greenish flowers which hang
in large numbers on the upright stem. Note the long
hanging green lip of the flower which is forked giving it
a somewhat sinister look but here the insects land and
then follow the nectar trail. Twayblade is a rhizomatous
perennial and its seeds need four years of mycorhizal
support before they can support themselves and then
another ten years before flowering. This mycorhizal
support is a symbiotic association between a fungus and
plants roots where there is a bi-directional movement of
nutrients benefiting both fungus and plant. Twayblade's
name is Listera ovata, Listeria being the name of a 17th
century palaeontologist, a Dr.M.Lister, and ovate which is
Latin for oval. The plant grows to a height of 30cms and
will flower from April to July.

Wood Sage

The wrinkled leaves look like Sage, hence its name.
This member of the mint family is found in a variety of
habitats but not necessarily in woods. The photograph
shows this specimen growing on a road verge. The
green and white flowers grow on one side of the stem
and at first glance may seem uninteresting but a closer
look will reveal a neat flower with the lower lip marked
with red. It has been used as a herb but does not have
the pungency of the culinary herb Sage as we know,
but it does have a similar aroma to the Hop and has the
attribute of clarifying beer quickly. The result is a liquid
with a rich dark colour. It has an old folklore name of
Hind Heal. Sick animals were thought to be cured of a
variety of ailments including blindness, and mixed with
horse feed would kill their worms, but the horse must not
drink for ten hours after it. The plant flowers from July to
September.

Bibliography

The Encyclopedia of Wild Flowers. 1999, Akeroyd John. Parragon, Bath.

Field Guide to the Wold Flowers of Britain and Northern Europe, 1996, Sutton John, Larousse plc, London.

Herbs and Healing Plants, 2012. Podlech Dieter. Harper Collins Publishers Ltd. London.

http://en.wikipedia.org/wki/

Plants of the British Isles, 1982, Nicholson Barbara, Peerage Books, London.

Readers Digest, Field Guide to the Wold Flowers of Britain, 1981, The Readers Digest Association Ltd. London.

Wild Flowers and where to find them in Northern England, Volumes 1, 2 and 3, 2004, Fallows Laurie, Frances Lincoln Ltd. London.

Index